From **PAVLOV'S DOGS** to **RORSCHACH'S INKBLOTS**,
put psychology's most fascinating theories to the test

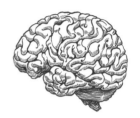

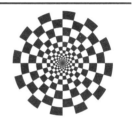

MICHAEL A. BRITT, PнD

# PSYCH
# EXPERIMENTS

T0039641

## Adams Media
New York   London   Toronto   Sydney   New Delhi

Adams Media
An Imprint of Simon & Schuster, Inc.
100 Technology Center Drive
Stoughton, MA 02072

For information about special discounts for bulk purchases, please contact Simon & Schuster Special Sales at 1-866-506-1949 or business@simonandschuster.com.

The Simon & Schuster Speakers Bureau can bring authors to your live event. For more information or to book an event contact the Simon & Schuster Speakers Bureau at 1-866-248-3049 or visit our website at www.simonspeakers.com.

Interior images © Dejan Bozic/123RF and by Claudia Wolf

Manufactured in the United States of America

7 2023

Library of Congress Cataloging-in-Publication Data has been applied for.

ISBN 978-1-4405-9707-7
ISBN 978-1-4405-9708-4 (ebook)

This book is intended as general information only, and should not be used to diagnose or treat any health condition. In light of the complex, individual, and specific nature of health problems, this book is not intended to replace professional medical advice. The ideas, procedures, and suggestions in this book are intended to supplement, not replace, the advice of a trained medical professional. Consult your physician before adopting any of the suggestions in this book, as well as about any condition that may require diagnosis or medical attention. The author and publisher disclaim any liability arising directly or indirectly from the use of this book.

Many of the designations used by manufacturers and sellers to distinguish their products are claimed as trademarks. Where those designations appear in this book and Simon & Schuster, Inc., was aware of a trademark claim, the designations have been printed with initial capital letters.

# CONTENTS

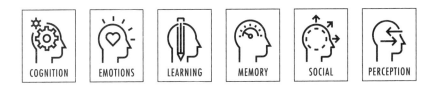

COGNITION   EMOTIONS   LEARNING   MEMORY   SOCIAL   PERCEPTION

# INTRODUCTION

Believe it or not, you do experiments pretty often in your day-to-day life. You may not call them that, and they may not fit the classic definition, but whenever you try to find out *why* something happened you are setting up an experiment. For example, imagine you get sick. You decide to figure out which food you ate yesterday made you sick. So you look for something that stands out—something unusual that you don't do every day. You think you've identified the offending food (at least you have a hypothesis), and so you decide that today you're going to keep everything the same in your diet except for that one thing. You're going to eliminate the possibilities. Congratulations, you're a scientist!

The only difference between you and a classic "scientist" is that what you do every day is a little "messy" scientifically speaking. You don't have control groups and impartial observers, you don't clearly define or measure your variables, and you don't run any statistics, but all these methods used by scientists are designed to do one thing: make us more careful observers so we can answer the "why" question with more confidence.

You may not carry out all of the studies described in this book, and that's okay, because you're still going to learn a lot about human behavior along the way. But if you do, I think you're going to have fun and learn a lot. Almost all the big names in the history of psychological experimentation are here: Pavlov, Skinner, Rorschach, Festinger, Piaget, Kohlberg, and Asch, along with other, more recent names like Seligman, Loftus, Cialdini, and Zimbardo. And you'll be introduced to some of the very latest research being conducted right now by psychologists like Barrett, Eastwick, Diehl, Wiseman, and Ariely.

Psychological research is very much alive and well and far from being something that's only done in "ivy towers." Psychological research is happening on websites (see the "curiosity effect"), in restaurants (see entry on how to increase your tips), in the courtroom (see entries on false memories and new lie detector tests), in advertisements (you'd be surprised how much you're influenced by the color red), and even right on your smartphone (why you are addicted to it and whether or not taking photos with it detracts from your real-life experience).

You'll be surprised to learn what psychologists are up to these days. But as I said, even if you don't carry out a single experiment or demonstration described in this book, I think you'll find that experimenting is actually kind of intriguing. You're like Sherlock Holmes when you conduct an experiment. You survey all the evidence looking for clues (in this case, clues about the "why" of human behavior) and then you try something to see what happens. And after all, isn't that what scientists and all curious people do? They try things to see what will happen.

So try a few things in this book and see what happens . . .

# CHAPTER 1

## AN INTRODUCTION TO PSYCH EXPERIMENTS

Salivating dogs, confused cats, superstitious pigeons, insightful gorillas, aggressive children, fearful adults—the list of fascinating psychological studies goes on and on. Research on humans is colorful, odd, brilliant, embarrassing, and sometimes difficult to watch. We have learned a lot and we have come a long way since Wilhelm Wundt (the "founder" of psychology back in 1879) had participants listening to metronomes tick and introspecting on the experience. Today we have sophisticated personality tests and MRI (magnetic resonance imaging) scans to look "inside the black box" of the brain while it thinks. But just because some research is "old"—like B. F. Skinner's work with pigeons—doesn't mean it's "old fashioned" or wrong. It's still quite useful. And just because we're using an MRI scan on our brains doesn't necessarily mean we understand what we're looking at. We look back at Sigmund Freud's work and think about how silly some of it was. But a hundred years from now we'll look back at what we're doing today and think the same thing.

## WHY PSYCH EXPERIMENTS MATTER

In this book we'll take a look at some of the most famous and some of the lesser-known studies in the history of psychology. I think you'll find it fun even if you never carry out any of the studies described here. Here are a few examples of the odd, the brilliant, and the important studies (some of which we'll re-create in this book).

### THE ODD
What if you showed up to assist an experimenter and he said that your job was to sit in a men's bathroom stall and videotape men as

they stand at a urinal and pee? Yes, that study was actually carried out in the 1970s by R. Dennis Middlemist and his colleagues. Sounds odd, but they wanted to see what effect it has on us to have someone else nearby when we're . . . eliminating. Not surprisingly perhaps, it does take longer for the "onset of micturition (peeing)" to occur when someone is nearby. You probably refer to this as an "invasion of your personal space." This study, while indeed a little odd, has been enormously helpful to people who suffer from shy bladder syndrome.

### THE SURPRISING

Many people fear the end of the world. Sometimes they even have a specific date (remember December 12, 2012, when the world was supposed to come to an end?). What goes on in people's minds when they very strongly believe something like this and then the world doesn't come to an end? How do they deal with it? Leon Festinger and his colleagues decided to actually join an "end of the world" cult to find out what happened on that last day. This study taught us a lot about an idea called *cognitive dissonance*. As you'll see in this book, cognitive dissonance is at work almost every day in your life.

### THE BRILLIANT

Not many studies can claim to have been inspired by a Bible story, but John M. Darley and C. Daniel Batson's study did just that. They took the parable of the Good Samaritan and turned it into a psychological study. The parable describes several people who walked by a man who was clearly in need of help. Many people did not help. One did. So Darley set up a study in which participants (who were seminary students) were asked to give a brief talk about this parable. But wouldn't you know it—participants had to walk to a building across campus to give the talk. And along the way, Darley and Batson placed a person on the ground who pretended to be in need of help. We learned a lot about situations in which helping does and doesn't happen and what to do to get help when you need it.

## THE INFLUENTIAL

Many of us believe our memories to be accurate. We think we have "flashbulb memories" and we think that because we "saw it with our own eyes!" it must have happened just the way we recall it. Psychologist Elizabeth Loftus showed us just how inaccurate and easily influenced our memories can be. She showed participants recordings of car accidents and then later asked them what they saw. A simple change in wording was all that was needed to make people believe that they saw things that weren't there or that did not happen. This research has been very influential (though perhaps not as much as psychologists would like) in the courts today when jurors examine evidence and come to their decisions.

## CONCEPTUAL REPLICATIONS

We're not going to be carrying out a replication of Stanley Milgram's research in which many participants actually believed that they were giving someone a lethal level of electric shock. Nor will we be locking participants into false jail cells and assigning them to roles of "Prisoner" and "Guard" (Philip Zimbardo). We won't be delivering small electric shocks to dogs (Martin Seligman), entering ourselves into psychiatric facilities (David Rosenhan), or running rats in a maze or shaping the behavior of pigeons (Skinner). Nonetheless, we can still learn about the power of conformity, social roles, labeling, shaping, and helplessness by carrying out what are called "conceptual replications." That is, we can still examine these important ideas by doing small studies that are different from the original ones but that could still demonstrate the existence of the phenomenon.

For example, we'll be looking at these concepts, but we'll be doing so in original ways:

- **Cognitive Dissonance:** Instead of following cult members around, we'll look at how dissonance occurs when you shop online.

- **Social Roles:** Instead of creating a mock prison as Zimbardo did, we'll see how social roles affect us when we're just working as a group in a class discussion.
- **Learned Helplessness:** Instead of giving small shocks to dogs as Seligman did, we'll examine the effects of helplessness by asking participants to solve anagrams—some of which are really hard to figure out.
- **Rorschach Inkblots:** Instead of giving inkblots to people to see if their interpretations of them indicate schizophrenia, we'll examine the difficulty of scoring these inkblots by showing them to participants and assigning unusual names to the responses.
- **Detecting Lies:** You probably don't have a polygraph machine lying around, but we can still explore how lies can be detected using a fun "story telling" approach.
- **Behavior Modification:** I'm going to assume that you also don't have access to a "Skinner box" and a bunch of pigeons. Nevertheless, you can still experience the idea of behavior modification using a piano keyboard (you'll find out).

## RESPECT YOUR PARTICIPANTS

Even though the replications described here should be fun, if there's one issue psychologists are fanatical about it is the care and respect for those people who agree to participate in our studies. For example, every college and university has an internal review board (IRB)—a group of people who read a proposal for every research study a psychologist would like to carry out. The IRB makes sure that these key components are a part of every study:

- **Informed Consent:** Every participant should be provided with enough information about the study to make a decision as to whether or not they wish to participate.
- **Freedom to Withdraw:** No one is ever forced, fooled, or coerced into participating in a psychological study. While many colleges

and universities require Psychology 101 students to participate in research as a learning experience, those below the age of eighteen and those who simply do not wish to participate have the option of doing an alternative assignment (such as writing a short paper on a topic of their interest).

- **Debriefing and Follow-Up:** Once the study is over, all participants are entitled to know exactly what the study was about, how to find out the results if they're interested, and who to contact if they have any questions or concerns about their participation in the study. Some studies, in order to really find what they're looking for, require some amount of deception or at least leaving out important information so that participants will act in as natural a way as possible. However, once the study is done, everything is explained to the participants.

## IS IT ETHICAL?

As investigators of human behavior, researchers must weigh the potential to learn something very important against the potential for risk to participants. This is the "ethical dilemma" that the IRB must assess when they read a proposal.

### RISKS

What are the potential risks to participants? In addition to risks of bodily harm, could participants suffer undue stress during the study? Is it possible that they'll leave the study feeling bad about themselves? Anxious? Sad? Ideally, we want participants to leave the study with a positive feeling about having contributed to our understanding of the human condition. But any study could stir up emotions in participants that the researchers (that's you) didn't anticipate. Some situations have obvious concerns, such as research on childhood abuse in which you're going to ask people questions about their pasts that they might not want to think about. Other situations are more subtle. Suppose you're interested in memory and you ask people to memorize words on a list. Sounds harmless, but some subjects might do poorly on the task and if they're older, they might begin to worry about whether they're coming down with Alzheimer's disease because they had a parent who had it. This is one reason debriefing and follow-up contact info are always provided to participants in case they have concerns or worries that pop up later on.

### BENEFITS

What are the benefits to humankind of this research? Typically, an IRB will focus on seeing if the risks to your participants are minimal. However, some risk might not be unavoidable, such as when research-ers try out a new drug and don't know exactly which dosage is best or what the side effects could be. In cases like this, IRB members have to ask themselves, "Are we going to learn something here that is so impor-tant that it's worth such risks?" It's an important and difficult question.

## PSYCHOLOGY STUDIES AND ETHICAL DILEMMAS

Here are some examples of studies with some obvious and some not-so-obvious dilemmas:

### MILGRAM'S STUDY OF AUTHORITY

Will people obey an authority figure even if it means seriously hurting another person? You have probably heard of the study con-ducted by Stanley Milgram in which participants, instructed to act as "teachers," gave shocks to "learners" when learners gave the wrong answer to questions. The study gave us some unsettling news about human beings and how we can do some hurtful things to others when told to do so by an authority figure. We also learned how and when blind obedience to authority can be decreased. Of course, no one was shocked in the Milgram study. The learners' yells of pain were pretend and they were recorded so that every participant heard the exact same recording. But still, this was a study that left many of the participants shaken to say the least. It was one of the studies that led to the establishment of the APA Code of Ethics. The study took place in the early 1960s and it was thought that while the findings were important, the study would never be replicated because of the potential for psychological harm to the participants. However, psychologist Jerry Burger came up with an ingenious way to replicate the study while significantly reducing the risks to participants. He looked carefully at Milgram's research and found that 79 percent of the "teachers" who gave the "learner" a shock of 150 volts went all the way to giving 450 volts (a voltage level labeled XXX on the "shock machine"). So 150 volts was something of a turning point. If you were willing to go that far you would probably go all the way. So what if we replicate the study but stop at the 150-volt point? Why go any further? Burger's IRB committee agreed to this thinking and the famous Milgram study was replicated in 2009. Burger provided a more extensive debriefing of his participants than Milgram did and the participants experienced much less stress. Unfortunately, it appears that not much has changed in the human psyche since Milgram's time: Burger also found that about two-thirds of his participants did what they were told to do by an authority figure and administered 150 volts. Blind obedience to authority is apparently still with us.

### FRUSTRATION AND CREATIVITY

Does frustration help people become more creative? Perhaps you've found yourself in a frustrating situation and it actually caused you to find a creative solution to the problem. So it's a reasonable question: does frustration (and how does frustration) cause us to be more creative? To answer this we would have to frustrate some participants. Hmm . . . How do you frustrate people? You could:

1. Ask them to do a task that isn't actually possible to complete
2. Give them false information such as telling them they did very poorly on a task (when actually they did as well as anyone else)

3. Tell students that their class schedules were lost and they have to sign up for everything all over again (this was actually proposed at one university I attended)

What we have to do is find a way to frustrate subjects that does not cause too much stress, but which will still allow us to examine what we're interested in (creativity in this case). See the chapter titled "How Does Creativity Really Work?" to learn one way researchers figured out how to do this.

## VIRTUALLY FIGHTING FEAR

Can virtual reality (VR) headsets be used to treat phobias? Suppose you have a fear of heights (most of us do, and for good reason), but you want to overcome it because your new job requires you to be in high places often. Well, one approach to treating phobias like this is called *flooding*, which in this case would involve your therapist actually taking you to a high building and asking you to stand near the edge. You'll be anxious, perhaps for quite a while, but eventually your anxiety will subside. Previous research has already demonstrated the effectiveness of this technique. But today we have virtual reality headsets. A reasonable question is, would it be equally effective to have a client wear these glasses and stand at the edge of a virtual building? Would this help cure the phobia? A research study on this sounds pretty straightforward: get yourself some VR headsets, hire a VR programming expert to create an "edge of the building" simulation, advertise that you're looking for participants who have a fear of heights to try a new kind of treatment, and see if you can have someone successfully overcome their fear of heights using the head gear. This sounds safer than having them actually stand at the edge of a building where they could fall. However, you'll want to realize that many people find the experience of wearing a VR headset not only disorienting, but literally sickening. How are you going to protect participants who may not yet be aware of this tendency?

## POSITIVE POSTS AND POSITIVITY

If you see positive posts on Facebook, are you more likely to post more positive posts yourself? You may have heard that back in 2012 researchers at Facebook conducted a study in which they showed some people mostly positive posts in their Facebook News Feed while other people saw more negative posts. They wanted to see if reading positive posts would make people feel more positive and then write positive posts themselves. Over 700,000 people had their Facebook feeds manipulated in this way. They found out that doing this manipulation of the News Feed didn't have a strong effect on people. But was it ethical? You might think it's relatively harmless, but what if slightly depressed persons started seeing lots of depressing posts? Could this make them more depressed? A review board, if given the chance to review this study before it was carried out, would have insisted on informed consent. Facebook might contend that when you agree to their terms of service you have consented to these sorts of manipulations. You might argue that, realistically, very few people actually read the terms of service for any online site they visit. What's the right thing to do?

## THE "SCIENCE-Y" STUFF

Student or teachers of psychology have probably noticed that I have avoided the use of many terms students learn in their classes about research methods in psychology—terms like independent and dependent variables, operational definitions, and control variables, as well as terms that deal with the details of statistical analysis. This was done so that this book can be enjoyed by a non-academic audience. However, all of the experiments described in this book can be carried out, the data analyzed, and report summaries written up. The variables—both independent (what is manipulated) and dependent (what is measured)—should not be hard to identify.

The data for most of these studies is in the form of what are referred to as "Likert scales." This means your participants circle a number on a scale from 1 to 5, 7, or 10. When this is the case and the study involves two groups of participants, the proper statistical test would be a between-groups t-test (no within-groups designs are described here). Some studies include three groups, and in this case a between-subjects ANOVA (analysis of variance) would be called for. When the response from your participants is in the form of yes/no, then a chi-square test is called for. Conducting statistical tests isn't necessary, however, and in most cases students can simply calculate averages and put the results in a bar chart.

None of the studies described in this book are done in a way that would eliminate all conceivable extraneous variables, so of course, if an analysis of the data is conducted, it's not certain that you will find a statistically significant result. In research, a significant result is never (and should never be) guaranteed. If you conduct a test and don't find a significant result, perhaps an extraneous variable got in the way. Or perhaps the original study got it wrong and you've found that the effect you're looking for actually doesn't exist. In that case, you might want to see if you can get your study published!

Okay, enough background information. Are you ready? Then let's do some experimenting!

# CLASSICAL CONDITIONING YOU CAN DO YOURSELF

## MAYBE WE'RE NOT SO DIFFERENT FROM DOGS AFTER ALL

**PSYCH CONCEPT:** Classical Conditioning
**NAME OF EXPERIMENT:** The Work of the Digestive Glands
**ORIGINAL SCIENTIST/RESEARCH:** Ivan P. Pavlov (1897/1902)

LEARNING

Aside from Sigmund Freud, Ivan Pavlov is the most well-known figure in psychology. Who has not heard about his famous salivating dogs? Many people think that what Pavlov did can only be done with dogs, but that's not so. Classical conditioning happens in humans as well. In this experiment we'll see that we can condition people to a stimulus that used to have absolutely no effect at all on them.

First, a little clarification about Pavlov's work: Pavlov was not a psychologist. He was a physiologist and was mainly interested in digestion. In his studies with dogs he was specifically interested in the salivation reflex. When we put food in our mouths we automatically release saliva as part of the digestive process, and he wanted to understand this process more fully.

Pavlov's work focused on bodily actions that are typically automatic, and he showed how these reactions can be learned. This is not to be confused with actions that are learned by being rewarded. For example, your dog may walk to you after you trained it to do so by giving it a treat when it came to you. Learning that occurs in response to some kind of reward is referred to by psychologists as *operant conditioning*.

## THE ORIGINAL EXPERIMENT

To make sure we have all the pieces of Pavlov's study in our heads, let's briefly go over what he did. First, Pavlov did a little surgery to implant a small tube (similar in size to a test tube) into the cheek of each dog. The tube collected and measured the dog's saliva. Then he put his dogs on a table and in a harness so they wouldn't walk away. Finally, he presented his dogs with a powder made from meat (not an actual steak as you might have heard). You can find images of the setup online by simply doing a search on the terms "pavlov dog setup."

Pavlov fully expected the dogs to salivate in response to the meat powder placed in front of them. What he didn't expect was what he noticed next: the dogs salivated when they heard his assistant with the meat powder walk up the stairs to the laboratory. It's a good thing Pavlov kept a keen eye on what was happening in his lab and noticed this. Once he saw it he decided to see if he could bring about salivation in response to other events.

So here's what he did. He put the dogs on the table and in the harness. Then he started a metronome. We think of Pavlov using bells but he didn't actually use a bell at first. Instead, he wanted a  sound that dogs had never heard before—a "neutral stimulus"—so he used a metronome. In Pavlov's time metronomes were wound up and made clicking sounds as the pendulum slowly swung from right to left.

At first, the dogs probably looked at the metronome curiously and then looked away. Then, just before giving the dogs a plate of the meat powder Pavlov started the metronome. He performed this pairing a number of times. Then he simply turned on the metronome and watched. Sure enough, saliva started to drip into the tubes. The dogs had made an association. They had learned something and did it in a very predictable, scientifically observable way. There was a lot of excitement about his findings, and justifiably so.

## LET'S TRY IT!

Typical demonstrations of classical conditioning (often also referred to as "Pavlovian conditioning") involve asking someone to put on a poncho or a plastic garbage bag. The teacher then reads a list of words to the student. Every time a specific "key word" on the list is spoken (for example the word "chair"), the teacher sprays the student with water. Of course, the student flinches from the spray of water. After many repetitions, the student flinches to the sound of the word "chair," even if the teacher decides not to spray the person after saying the word. And that's all there is to it really. In this example the word "chair" is a neutral stimulus at first. Then through repeated pairings with the water (the unconditioned stimulus) the person flinches in response to the word "chair." The word "chair" is now a conditioned (or trained) stimulus, and the flinching in response to the word is the conditioned response. Voilà! Pavlov at work.

Here's another fun way to try out Pavlov's ideas. You'll need:

- Two dice
- Dice cup
- Horn—preferably a really loud and annoying one
- Table where you and your participants can sit
- A place where a loud noise isn't going to bother anyone

To make this an experiment you'll need two groups of people. We'll call them group A and B.

## WHAT TO DO:

### GROUP A

- **STEP 1:** Sit your subjects at a table and have the dice in the cup and your horn ready.
- **STEP 2:** Tell members of group A that you're going to roll the dice and if the dice add up to an even number you're going to blast the horn. If the number is odd, no horn. Make sure that the horn is loud enough to make your subjects wince.
- **STEP 3:** Shake the dice in the cup and then roll your dice and sound the horn when the criteria are met.
- **STEP 4:** Repeat this about a dozen times.

### GROUP B

- **STEP 1:** Again, sit your subjects at your table and have your materials ready.
- **STEP 2:** Tell this group that you'll only sound the horn if the dice add up to less than 6.
- **STEP 3:** Put the dice in the cup and shake it, roll the dice onto the table, and sound the horn when the criteria are met.
- **STEP 4:** Repeat a dozen times.

## THE RESULTS

What you're doing is conditioning your subjects to wince when you shake the dice. At first, shaking the dice is a neutral stimulus. That is, in your first few shakes of the cup you won't see any reaction from your participants. In group A, however, you'll be hitting that horn almost every time you roll the dice and they'll get conditioned to wincing when you shake the cup. Group B probably will not wince to the sight and sound of shaking the cup because the connection to the horn sound is very weak. In a way, the shaking of the cup is similar to Pavlov's assistant walking up the stairs.

Classical Conditioning You Can Do Yourself

## WHY IT MATTERS

If you're observant you'll see Pavlov's principles at work in your life. Are you or anyone you know uncomfortable when you go to the hospital—even to visit someone? That's because the sights, sounds, and smells of hospitals have become associated with anxiety. The classic example of Pavlovian conditioning in everyday life is the dentist's drill. The sound is neutral at first, but the more often you have dental work and experience the drill (which is sometimes painful), the more likely it is that you'll wince even when you just see that darn drill.

# HOW YOU ARE MANIPULATED INTO PAYING MORE MONEY THAN YOU WANTED

## I'LL BET YOU EXPECTED TO PAY THOUSANDS FOR THIS!

**PSYCH CONCEPT:** Anchoring

**NAME OF EXPERIMENT:** "Coherent Arbitrariness": Stable Demand Curves Without Stable Preferences

**ORIGINAL SCIENTIST/RESEARCH:** Dan Ariely, George Loewenstein, and Drazen Prelec (2003)

SOCIAL

The title of this research probably sounds pretty daunting, but every time you go to a store or shop online you are probably being influenced by what these researchers found. Here's an example: have you ever shopped for a mobile app? The typical app in either iTunes or Google Play is either free or just a dollar or two. What if you came across an app that cost $5.99? Wow—you'd probably think that's expensive. But think about it—six dollars? You could easily spend that amount on a soda and a couple slices of pizza. And that's the point: what you think of as expensive or cheap isn't some objective standard you carry around in your head. What you think of as expensive or cheap often depends on how much products cost that you just heard about or looked at.

This is why you'll hear an advertiser tell you what you would "expect to pay" for a product and then give you what is still a very high price. Let's say you're watching an ad on TV for the latest calorie-burning fitness equipment. The advertiser would like to sell the equipment for $300. You probably don't have any expectations regarding the price of this piece of equipment but the advertiser will suggest that "you would probably expect to pay $600 for a product like this" and that "some stores sell this for $500." When the price of $300 is finally given you're likely to think that $300 is a darn good price.

Another example: when you're shopping for a car the dealer will ask you how much you're looking to spend. Let's say that you're looking to find a car for no more than $15,000. The dealer will start by showing you cars that cost a lot more than that—perhaps $25,000. The dealer is trying to psychologically set what's called a high "anchor." The anchor is a price you will use in your mind when you look at every other car. The next step in this influence process is to show you cars that are a little bit lower than the expensive one but still higher than what you would like to spend. If the dealer is successful with this technique you would wind up thinking that a car of $18,000 is a darn good buy.

You've just been manipulated by the anchoring effect.

## THE ORIGINAL EXPERIMENT

You would be amazed at how easy it is to manipulate people with this technique. Dan Ariely and his colleagues were able to manipulate people's sense of how much they would pay for a product using anchor numbers that had nothing at all to do with the product itself. First they picked products that people weren't that familiar with, such as cordless trackpads, keyboards, and a box of Belgian chocolates. Do you have any idea how much these products typically cost? You probably have a wide range of prices in mind—anywhere from, say, $10 to $100. As it turns out, Ariely chose products with an average price of about $70.

So how do I get you to be willing to pay a price that's as high as possible? Ariely used the anchoring manipulation but he didn't do what the TV advertiser did by telling you the prices of "similar products." Instead, he simply asked people whether they would be willing to buy these products for the amount that is equal to the final two digits of their social security number. They were also asked for the maximum amount they would be willing to pay for the products.

Guess what? Participants whose last two digits of their social security number were low (below the median) gave prices that were low, and participants whose social security numbers were high (above the median) gave high prices! So simply being reminded of your social security number—which of course has nothing to do with the price of these products—was enough to influence how much participants were willing to pay for a product. For example, participants who had social security numbers in which the last two digits were high numbers were willing to pay an average of $57 for the cordless keyboard. Those with social security numbers ending in low numbers were only willing to pay about $16!

## LET'S TRY IT!

You could have a little fun with this effect. Here's what you'll need:

- Group of friends
- Index cards (equal to number of participants)
- Five images of products most people are not familiar with

### WHAT TO DO:

- **STEP 1:** Tell your friends you're doing a little research for school or that you're just interested in what they think of some new products you're thinking of buying yourself.
- **STEP 2:** Get your index cards and on each card write down on the left side of the card either a low number (lower than 20) or a high number (higher than 80 and up to 100).
- **STEP 3:** Before you start your experiment, give each participant one of the index cards on which you wrote a number (ask them not to show their number to anyone else if you're doing this study in a group setting). If they're curious about this number, just tell them that you're going to look at their information later but you want it to be anonymous, which is why you gave each of them a random "identity number."

- **STEP 4:** Tell your participants that you're going to show them some products and ask them to write down on the right side of the card the name of the product and the *maximum* price they'd be willing to pay for it.
- **STEP 5:** Show them—one at a time—images of the products. Feel free to use the same products the researchers used—cordless keyboards, expensive chocolates, a rare bottle of wine, etc. If they want a lot of details about each product tell them that they have to make their decision based only on what they see in the image.
- **STEP 6:** Give them 2 minutes maximum to look at the image of the product and write down the answer on the right side of the card.

## THE RESULTS

The experiment is over once you have shown them your last product. Gather the cards and take a look at the info you've collected. I'll bet you'll find that those who received low "identity numbers" came up with prices that are lower than those who received high numbers. If you're doing this experiment in a group format you could even have some fun and let your participants show their index cards to each other and take a look at the results themselves. An interesting conversation could come out of this.

## WHY IT MATTERS

This "anchoring manipulation" is used in many areas of life to try to persuade you to pay more for a product than you might initially be willing to pay. So as usual, "buyer beware." The only way to protect yourself against this is to do your research before coming into a buying situation. This is especially true when you're buying a car. Look through the various car-buying resources either online or in print so that you know how much the car you're interested in should cost. If these sources say that the car you're interested in typically goes for, say, $17,000, then make this number your own anchor and compare other cars against it. Don't let the dealer or the text in an advertisement sway you into thinking anything different. When you're shopping for a mobile app remember that $3.99 is not a high price just because other apps nearby are going for free. Step back mentally and look at what you're getting for the price. When you shop online, remember that some very expensive products are placed in front of you on the webpage with no expectation that you'll actually buy them. They are there to set a high anchor. The seller fully expects you to scroll down the page and find a product that is a little bit cheaper than the expensive one—but probably still a good deal more than you wanted to spend.

# ESTIMATING DISTANCES—MORE PSYCHOLOGY THAN YOU THINK

## *FEAR CAN CORRUPT YOUR BRAIN'S ABILITY TO MEASURE*

**PSYCH CONCEPT:** Perception

**NAME OF EXPERIMENT:** The Roles of Altitude and Fear in the Perception of Height

**ORIGINAL SCIENTIST/RESEARCH:** Jeanine K. Stefanucci and Dennis R. Proffitt (2010)

A lot of people have a fear of heights, and evolutionarily speaking that's probably a good thing; after all, usually only those humans who were afraid of heights survived. But did you know that your perception of how far away things are (and your resulting fear) depends on where you're standing at the time you're asked? There's a body of research around this idea called *evolved navigation*. For example, suppose you stood at the bottom of a building and looked up toward the roof. Then suppose you were at the top of that same building looking down to the ground. Do you think you would estimate the height of a building differently from these two positions? Turns out you would.

## THE ORIGINAL EXPERIMENT

Researchers Jeanine Stefanucci and Dennis Proffitt did an experiment that, with a little modification, you could try yourself.

Here's what they did. They took a building on their college campus that had a balcony running along the outside that people could stand on. The balcony was about 26 feet (8 meters) high. Some participants were asked to stand at the edge of the balcony (with the railing in front of them to prevent falling) and look down at the ground. They were asked to look at a round flat disc on the ground and estimate how far it was from the top of the railing down to the disc. Other participants did this same task but they were standing on the ground looking up at the disc, which was placed at the top of the railing. So the actual physical distance from the person to the disc was exactly the same each time. How did the participants' point of view affect their distance estimates?

As you might have guessed, looking down at the ground from a height created a little sense of fear and caused the participants to estimate that the distance to the ground was much farther than if they had been standing on the ground looking up. Participants who were looking down thought that the distance was about 41 feet (12.5 meters) to the ground. Those looking up thought the balcony was about 31 feet (9.5 meters) away.

So if you've ever wondered if we see reality the way it really is, it looks like we don't. Our perceptions do indeed depend on where we're literally standing at the time.

## LET'S TRY IT!

You could do this study yourself by finding a tall spot where your friends can stand and ask them to estimate how many feet (or meters) it is from their feet to the ground. Have another group of friends stand at ground level and look up (to the point where a person's feet would be if they were standing up there). Ask them to estimate how high that point is. You'll probably find that those looking down think it is much farther away than those looking up.

However, these researchers also discovered another aspect of perception that is a little safer to test. It turns out that people also overestimate a distance if they think it'll take a lot of physical effort to get there. So, if you're outside and looking across a lot of rough terrain (lots of rocks and small hills), you'll think it's farther to the other side than if you were looking across a flat terrain—even if the two distances are exactly the same. This experiment will be much easier to test and doesn't require positioning your friends up on a high building. Here's what you'll need:

- 2–4 friends
- Large parking lot (or other vast terrain)
- Backpack filled with very heavy books

**WHAT TO DO:**

- **STEP 1:** Stand at one end of the parking lot and ask a friend or a few friends to estimate how many feet (or meters) it is to the other side of the lot. Make sure the participants can't hear each other's estimates.
- **STEP 2:** Turn to your second friend or friends, but before you ask this same question, have each put the backpack over his or her shoulders.

Will the added weight make your second friend think that the other side is a whole lot farther away?

## THE RESULTS

If Stefanucci and Proffitt are correct, the added weight will cause your participants to think that your target is even farther away than it really is. So participants with the heavy backpack will probably give you higher estimates—whether you asked for the number of feet or meters.

## WHY IT MATTERS

You could use this study as an example if you ever get into a discussion about whether the body and the mind are separate entities. They're not. As this study shows, sensations from our bodies do indeed affect the way we think.

It's also good to remember that if you are walking a long distance or running in a marathon you might think that the finish line is farther away if you're tired or you've got some hills in front of you.

# YOUR MEMORY IS BETTER THAN YOU THINK

## HOW AM I GOING TO REMEMBER ALL THAT?

**PSYCH CONCEPT:** Mnemonics
**NAME OF EXPERIMENT:** Memory: A Contribution to Experimental Psychology
**ORIGINAL SCIENTIST/RESEARCH:** Hermann Ebbinghaus (1885)

MEMORY

How many times have you sat in a lecture in which a lot of information was being presented and thought to yourself, "How am I ever going to remember all this stuff?" You know you can only carry a few bits of information in your short-term memory and for only a short while—perhaps a few days if you keep repeating the info to yourself. So you understandably don't have much confidence in how much you can remember. However, it could be you're just not using your memory to its full capacity. In this experiment I think you'll be surprised how much more you can remember than you expect. In fact, there are quite a few little "memory tricks" you probably don't know about. We'll explore them in this and other psychology experiments.

## THE ORIGINAL EXPERIMENT

The Greeks were fascinated with memory strategies thousands of years ago, but the first careful studies were conducted by Hermann Ebbinghaus in the mid-1800s. Interestingly, he decided to use himself as the subject in all his studies. Ebbinghaus was a very meticulous person, and his approach was pretty straightforward. He sat down and presented himself with lots and lots of words one after the other and then wrote down as many of these words as he could recall, both immediately after looking at them and also on the next day, the day after that, and the day after that.

Ebbinghaus didn't want to use random lists of ordinary words like "cat" or "bat" that would be easier to learn just because they were familiar. To solve that problem he came up with what he called "nonsense syllables": three-letter words that had a consistent pattern. They all started with a consonant. The next letter was a vowel and the last letter was another consonant. In this way he created words like "baj" or "juf."

Also, like any good scientific thinker he realized that he should look at each unfamiliar word for the exact same amount of time. In that day, musicians often used wind-up metronomes to provide a steady tick-tock rhythm, so Ebbinghaus used a metronome when he presented the words to himself to make sure that he didn't look at any word longer than another.

At first he was able to write down a lot of words correctly. Then he found that after about six days he could no longer remember any of the words. From this work he came up with the *forgetting curve* of memory, which helped us better understand exactly how short our short-term memories work.

George Miller picked up with Ebbinghaus's work in the 1950s. He focused on *memory span*, that is, the maximum number of items you can keep in your head immediately after you hear them. For example, if I said three random letters out loud, you would easily be able to repeat them immediately back to me. But how many more letters could I add before you start to feel unsure of yourself and make mistakes? Miller found that the human memory could hold only about seven items in short-term memory. Almost nobody could correctly repeat back ten random letters.

## LET'S TRY IT!

You could easily replicate Ebbinghaus's and Miller's work by simply asking someone to repeat letters back to you as you go from one to ten letters. You would find that people would start to make mistakes around seven letters. But let's do something that's more fun.

Researchers after Miller found out that there is a way to beat this seven-letter "limit." We can remember more than seven items if we can find a *pattern* to the things we're asked to remember. Let's take a look at some examples. Do you think you could repeat back all ten of these numbers?

7294682534

You would probably have trouble getting more than seven right because the numbers are pretty random. How about these numbers:

248163264128

You may have noticed that this list of numbers actually might not be that hard to remember. The first three digits are even numbers. But there's a deeper structure to the numbers: the numbers double as they go from left to right. With that knowledge in mind, I'll wager you could now look away and repeat all twelve numbers.

With this in mind let's replicate this study on memory. Here's what you'll need:

- Group of 2–4 friends
- Pen
- Index cards
- Stopwatch

**WHAT TO DO:**
- **STEP 1:** Write down the numbers 248163264128 on an index card
- **STEP 2:** Give the card to one friend or group of friends and ask them to look at the numbers for 15 seconds and then give the card back to you.

- **STEP 3:** Ask them to repeat back as many numbers as they can. Do this individually. Write down what each person says.
- **STEP 4:** Now give the same group of numbers to another friend or group of friends, but before you hand over the paper, inform them that there is a pattern to the numbers. (That hint will be all they need to detect when they look at them that the numbers double as they go from left to right.)
- **STEP 5:** Let them look at the card for 15 seconds and then give it back to you.
- **STEP 6:** Ask the second group of people individually to repeat back the numbers. Write down their answers.

## THE RESULTS

In this experiment you'll discover that the first group could probably only remember about seven numbers at most, and they could probably correctly tell you the first and last couple of numbers. This tendency to recall the first and last things we heard is called the primacy and recency effect. The second group of friends probably got all or most of the numbers right (if they were able to detect the pattern).

## WHY IT MATTERS

So you might be thinking that this is an interesting "parlor trick," but of what value is it in everyday life? What this tells us is that whenever you find or apply a pattern to what looks like random information, you will be more likely to recall that information. You probably already do this. For example, if someone's telephone number ends in, let's say, 8228, it's easier to remember than a number that ends in 9437. The numbers 8228 have an easily detectable pattern and they kind of rhyme, whereas it's hard to see a pattern in 9437. But what if you *created a pattern* for them? Let's break them into smaller numbers: 94 and 37. Do you know an old person who lived to be 94? How about a friend who got married at age 37? Did you ever have an address that included 94, 43, 37, 943, or 437? If you take a moment to play with the numbers and discover or apply a familiar association to them you will be surprised to find what you can do with your memory.

# HOW EYEWITNESSES CAN BE MISLED

## *YOUR MEMORY IS NOT NEARLY AS GOOD AS YOU THINK*

**PSYCH CONCEPT:** Eyewitness Testimony

**NAME OF EXPERIMENT:** Reconstruction of Automobile Destruction: An Example of the Interaction Between Language and Memory

**ORIGINAL SCIENTIST/RESEARCH:** Elizabeth F. Loftus and John C. Palmer (1974)

Most of us think we have pretty good memories. How many times have you heard someone (or yourself) say, "I know exactly where I was when XYZ happened." We know that we don't remember everything that happened to us in our lives, but when we have a vivid memory we think our brains recorded what happened in the exact manner that it happened. As it turns out, this is far from true. Despite our confidence in our memories, researchers have found that our memories often consist of bits and pieces of what actually happened along with bits and pieces of what we think *probably* happened. We construct a story in our minds as to what happened—a story that makes sense to us and to other people as we tell it. In other words, you put together a "memory story" from the bits and pieces—and not all of those pieces may have actually happened.

## THE ORIGINAL EXPERIMENT

Dr. Elizabeth Loftus has been studying eyewitness memory since the early 1970s, and her findings have had a big impact on judges and lawyers when they conduct their work with eyewitnesses. One of Dr. Loftus's most convincing studies on how fragile our memories are involved having subjects view a brief video of a car accident. All the participants saw the same clip and all them were then asked how fast they thought one car was going when the accident occurred. Sounds pretty straightforward so far.

What was different in the experiment was the *words* that were used to describe the speed of the car. In one group, the participants were asked how fast one car was going when it "smashed" into the other, while other participants were asked to estimate the speed of the cars when they "contacted" each other.

You might not be surprised to find out that on average, participants thought the cars were going about 40 mph when they were told the cars "smashed" into each other and only about 31 mph when told that they "contacted" each other. In other studies, Loftus asked subjects if they remember seeing "the broken glass," when there was no broken glass shown in the video. Guess what? A lot of subjects say that yes, they did indeed see the broken glass.

These studies show us that our perception of what we saw (the speed of the cars) and our memory of what we saw (broken glass) can be manipulated. And we will still feel confident about what we think happened.

Let's see if we can replicate the basic idea.

## LET'S TRY IT!

NOTE: this study will involve showing people a video of a car accident. Some participants may have actually been in a car accident or perhaps they know someone who was hurt or killed in one. Obviously, watching a video of even a simple car accident could stir up unpleasant memories. As always, respect participants' wishes if they do not want to participate.

To replicate Loftus's study you'll need:

- Video of a car accident
- Participants to watch the video
- Two pieces of paper with one (or two) questions printed on it: one piece of paper contains a question that asks subjects to estimate the speed of the cars "when they contacted each other," and the other piece of paper contains the same question except that it replaces "contacted" with "smashed into"

A brief video of a simple car accident would be fine. You can find videos like this on YouTube by simply searching on the term "car accident." However, it is hard to find a brief video of an accident and you certainly don't want to use a video that is disturbing to watch. The focus should be on a simple accident and not one with gory details. Feel free to use this video:

Car Accident Video (www.youtube.com/watch?v=_uZq5-Fb47o).

**WHAT TO DO:**

- **STEP 1:** Tell your participants that you'll be asking them to estimate the speed of two cars they'll see in a video.
- **STEP 2:** Hand out your pieces of paper. They're exactly the same except for one word: "smashed" versus "contacted" as previously described.
- **STEP 3:** Show the video.
- **STEP 4:** Don't allow any discussion.
- **STEP 5:** Ask participants to answer the question on their piece of paper.
- **STEP 6:** Optional: The previous YouTube video link shows an accident in which there is no stop sign visible. You could ask your subjects if they saw the stop sign—Yes, No, or Not Sure.

## THE RESULTS

You will likely find what Loftus found: that speed estimates are higher among those subjects who had the accident described with the word "smashed."

Feel free to talk to your participants about their reactions to the study. Are they as confident now about their memories as they were before your study?

## WHY IT MATTERS

Why would you want to look into this phenomenon? Well, at some point in your life you'll probably be required to sit on a "jury of your peers." Many if not all of those people will believe that their memories are quite good, and they will likely be swayed by the confidence with which eyewitnesses tell their stories about what they saw. When you serve on a jury you may be the one to help others understand how fragile our memories really are and to focus on the evidence that is strongest—and not on how confident witnesses believe themselves to be.

# YES—WALKING THROUGH A DOOR WILL CAUSE YOU TO FORGET

## NOW WHY DID I COME IN HERE?

**PSYCH CONCEPT:** Encoding and Forgetting

**NAME OF EXPERIMENT:** Walking Through Doorways Causes Forgetting: Situation Models and Experienced Space

**ORIGINAL SCIENTIST/RESEARCH:** Gabriel A. Radvansky and David E. Copeland (2006)

MEMORY

You've probably experienced this at some point: you're sitting in one room working on something or simply brushing your teeth and you're thinking that you need to go and get something. So you put down what you're doing and you go into another room and poof! You stand there in the new room and have no idea why you're there.

If this has happened to you, don't worry; you're not alone. Not only can many, many people identify with what happened to you, but scientists have experienced it as well and have conducted a number of studies to learn why it happened. They think they have some answers, and you can probably repeat their study right in your own home or office.

What we're looking at here is what memory researchers call *encoding* and what we all call "forgetting." Encoding is the idea of how we get information into our heads. Does it come in through our eyes? Ears? Where were we when we first heard or saw the information? What time of day was it? How much time did you spend getting the information into your head? All of these things have something to do with how well the information went into our heads and how well we can remember it a few minutes or a few days or even years afterward. The "walking through doorways" phenomenon explores how could it be that the event of simply walking from one room to another causes you to forget. It is called the *event model* of memory and it's actually not that complicated. Let's take a look.

## THE ORIGINAL EXPERIMENT

Imagine if you wanted to do studies on the effects of walking through doorways on a person's memory. Naturally, you would need to get your subjects walking and you would need several different rooms with doors between them. You could do this in the "real world" if you had a lot of space, but why not make use of computer technology and have your subjects do their walking in a virtual world? Using a virtual world has one advantage over real worlds that scientists really like: control over the environment. For example, if you used the real world and had your subjects walk from one end of a building to another you might not be able to control who your subjects ran into, who started a conversation with them, or what unexpected events they might see along the way. All of these uncontrolled events can affect their ability to remember. On the other hand, if you created a virtual world on a computer and put your subjects inside a setting with rooms and doors, and your subjects "walked" around these rooms using a mouse or trackpad, you would have total control over what happens as they do their walking. The "walking" is admittedly virtual, but in at least initial research that element of control is very important. Plus, perhaps, researchers are computer nerds at heart.

Radvansky and her colleagues decided to create their own virtual world with rooms and doors with the same game engine used to create the popular video game *Half-Life*. The "world" that Radvansky created is extremely simple compared to many of today's popular games (which sometimes cost millions to create) but, after all, we only need a few rooms and doors here for the subjects to "walk" through.

But what about the other important component of this phenomenon—the thing you need to remember when you go from one room to another? In the real world, you probably left one room and went into another because you needed to get your cell phone, get a certain book, or feed your cat. How are we going to re-create this idea in a virtual world? What Radvansky did was to give her subjects objects that they had to "pick up" as they moved from one room to another. The objects were quite simple things like geometric shapes: triangles or square-shaped. Subjects went over to a table and picked up an object. At that point the object disappeared from view, as if they had put the object into a bag they were carrying. Then they were instructed to walk over to a door, open it, and walk into another virtual room. When they arrived in the new room they were asked to remember what they had picked up in the previous room. Other subjects also picked up an object and walked the same amount of virtual space but did not have to open a door in the process.

Guess what happened? People who picked up an object and then walked into the next room and asked what they picked up in the previous room took longer to answer and were less often correct than people who picked up the same object and walked the same virtual distance but simply did not open a door in the process.

This is why Radvansky suggests that there is an "event" component to our memories. It seems that when we're in one physical space we can remember what we're doing there, but when an event occurs—that is, we go into a new room—our brain partially "empties" itself of what we did and what we were thinking about in the previous location. We're probably preparing more "space" in our memories to deal with what will happen in the new location.

## LET'S TRY IT!

Okay, so how can you replicate this—especially if you're not a computer game programmer like Radvansky? You can replicate this study the old-fashioned way by actually having your subjects do some walking. What you'll need is:

- You're going to be using a two-group design here, so it would be great to have 10 participants in each group for a total of 20 participants.
- Space with a few rooms separated by doors. You could use your house and designate your living room, den, and bedroom as your experimental space. (Try to keep the number of distractions to a minimum. Don't have the TV on and try to keep the area clear of people who might interact with your subjects.)
- Space that has a long hallway or rooms that are not separated by doors.
- 4 small objects for your subjects to carry in the backpack. (You don't want anything heavy. Examples might be an empty milk carton, a set of car keys, a small notepad, and an alarm clock.)
- 4 tables where you will place objects for your subjects to pick up.
- 4 large boxes with no tops that you'll put over the objects to hide them.
- Backpack or large piece of luggage
- Stopwatch
- Clipboard with a piece of paper for recording your data

**WHAT TO DO:**
Now let's take a look at your two conditions:

### GROUP A: WALKING THROUGH DOORWAYS
- **STEP 1:** In each of your rooms place 1 object on a table under a box so it is hidden.
- **STEP 2:** Have your participant start in a corner of the first of your rooms. Give him the backpack. Tell him to go over to the table, pick up the object under the box, and put it in the backpack. Then he should go over to the door, open it, and go into the next room.
- **STEP 3:** If you're the only one conducting this study you'll have to follow behind each subject as they walk from room to room. Be ready with a clipboard to record your subject's answer. Have your

stopwatch ready (at your side or behind your back). As soon as the participant comes into the next room ask him, "What are you carrying in your backpack?" As soon as you have finished asking the question start the stopwatch. As soon as your subject answers the question (right or wrong) stop the stopwatch. Write down on your clipboard:

1. The subject's number (1 through however many subjects you get to participate)
2. The room you're in ("room 1," "room 2," and so on)
3. The object your subject said was in the backpack
4. The exact amount of time it took your subject to give you an answer (down to hundredths of a second)

- **STEP 4:** Take the object out of the backpack and put it on the floor. Tell your subject to go into the next room and get the object from that table.

### GROUP B: WALKING, BUT NO DOORS

This condition is almost exactly like the previous one except that your subjects will not be walking through any doorways. Ideally, they will be walking a straight distance (and roughly the same amount of distance) from one table to the next. If that's not possible you'll still probably get the same results as Radvansky, even if your subjects have to take a few turns in the hallway.

- **STEP 1:** Place 4 tables in the hallway roughly the same distance from each other. On each table place 1 object under a box so it is hidden.
- **STEP 2:** Have your participant start at the end of the hallway. Give her the backpack. Tell her to go over to the first table, pick up the object under the box, and put it in the backpack. Then she should walk straight to the next table.

- **STEP 3:** Be ready with a clipboard to record your subject's answer. Have your stopwatch ready (at your side or behind your back). As soon as the participant gets to the next table ask her, "What are you carrying in your backpack?" As soon as you have finished asking the question start the stopwatch. As soon as your subject answers the question (right or wrong) stop the stopwatch. Write down on your clipboard:

  1. The subject's number (1 through however many subjects you get to participate)
  2. The table you are at ("table 2," "table 3," and so on)
  3. The object your subject said was in the backpack
  4. The exact amount of time it took your subject to give you an answer (down to hundredths of a second)

- **STEP 4:** Take the object out of the backpack and put it on the floor. Tell your subject to get the object from the next table.

## THE RESULTS

You may find that your subjects remember exactly what's in their backpack each time you ask, but you'll no doubt find that it takes them a bit longer to say what's in the backpack if they have just walked through a doorway. Your hallway subjects will probably look at you with a strange face when you repeatedly ask what to them is an obvious question, but you'll use their data as a comparison to your "doorway" subjects.

## WHY IT MATTERS

Scientists love to be able to replicate and explain things that happen in our daily lives, and this study does just that. When you explain what you did to your subjects I'll bet that many of them will nod their heads and say, "Oh yeah, that happened to me." You can explain a little about the event model of memory and they'll probably think that's a little interesting, but just having their daily experience supported by scientists is enough to impress many people. One bit of practical advice from this study is that if you're going to leave one room to go to do something in another, it would probably do you some good to repeat why you're going to that other room at least once or twice before you leave the room you're in. Repetition like this will put the information into your short-term memory for a longer period of time, prevent your brain from "emptying" its contents when you leave the room, and increase the chances you'll remember what the heck you came in here for!

# THE METHOD OF LOCI—ONE OF THE MOST POWERFUL MEMORY TECHNIQUES

## WOW—I CAN'T BELIEVE I REMEMBERED ALL OF THAT!

**PSYCH CONCEPT:** Memory—Method of Loci
**NAME OF EXPERIMENT:** Does the Repeated Use of Loci Create Interference?
**ORIGINAL SCIENTIST/RESEARCH:** Rossana De Beni and Cesare Cornoldi (1988)

MEMORY

Most of us are not aware of how many things we can actually remember. There are many memory techniques (called mnemonics) that most people just don't take advantage of. When you use them you'll be surprised how quickly you can memorize even a long list of things. The method of *loci*, first made famous by the Greeks, is a visual technique in which you picture in your mind the inside of a house or apartment and you picture the objects inside the house. These objects or "spots" inside the house are your "locations" (loci). For example, you could picture your kitchen. Each object in the kitchen would be one of your "loci." So, as you look from left to right in your kitchen perhaps you see a cabinet, the sink, the oven, the refrigerator, and so on. You could also imagine walking through your house and at each distinct location or object try to link the object to whatever it is you want to remember. Then, to remember the items later you simply "walk" through your house again and the associations you made to each object (or location in the house) will activate your memory. For this demonstration we'll use a list of foods to buy at the supermarket, but you can use this technique if you're in school and you have a lot to recall for a test.

## THE ORIGINAL EXPERIMENT

The method of loci was first developed by the Greeks thousands of years ago, but you can use an excellent experiment conducted by De Beni and Cornoldi as a starting place for your own experiment. One group of high school students was trained in how the loci method worked and then was given a long passage to read. The group members were asked to use the method to memorize the key points of the reading. Another group was given the same reading but they were not trained in how the method of loci worked. They were just asked to remember as much of the reading as they could using what most people do—repetition. Both groups were tested immediately after they finished reading and studying. They were also tested on the material one week later. Not surprisingly, the group that used the method of loci remembered much more than the repetition group.

## LET'S TRY IT!

Let's try out this memory technique on a few friends. First you'll need a list of things you want your friends to remember. Let's use the idea of having to go to the supermarket to pick up some groceries. Let's really stretch ourselves and make a list of ten items. You can make up whatever grocery items you want, but here's what I suggest:

1. Bread
2. Milk
3. Peanut butter
4. Broccoli
5. Cereal
6. Frozen pizza
7. Eggs
8. Cat (or dog) food
9. Toilet paper
10. Carrots

Here's what else you'll need:

- 2 groups of participants
- Paper with 10-item grocery list
- Blank paper for recording
- Stopwatch
- Pencil or pen

## WHAT TO DO:

### GROUP A: METHOD OF LOCI GROUP

- **STEP 1:** Tell the group A participants that you're going to ask them to memorize 10 items they might buy in a grocery store. You'll be giving them 5 minutes to look over the list. Have your stopwatch set for 5 minutes but don't start it yet.
- **STEP 2:** Explain the method of loci to them. When you're done explaining it, ask them to pick 10 "spots." The spots could be rooms in their house or apartment or places along the route to school or work. If they're picturing a house, have them "walk" through the house with you out loud, starting in the basement. Next to each grocery item have them write down a spot along their walk through their house. Here are a few spots they will probably choose (or you could suggest to them):

1. The garage.
2. Some spot in the basement like the oil burner or air conditioning unit. It has to be a specific spot—not just the corner of the basement for example.
3. The stairs that go up to the first floor.
4. An item in the room at the top of the stairs—if it's the kitchen, then the stove or fridge is a good object or spot.

5.  Go into the next room. What's there? Perhaps a TV? Does the room have a dining room table? Or a couch? You can certainly use more than one object per room.
6.  The stairs that go to the second floor.
7.  The room at the top of the stairs. If that room is a bathroom then choose the toilet or the bathtub.
8.  The next room is probably either a bedroom with a bed, closet, and window or a den with a desk and lamp.
9.  Go into the next room . . . You get the idea.

Continue until you have 10 unique spots in each participant's house or apartment. In the case of apartments that don't have a lot of rooms, participants can just use a number of objects in each room. For the kitchen they can use the fridge, the stove, the microwave, the sink, and a closet. Same thing for the living room—they probably have a couch, a side table, a window, a big chair, a TV, etc. Each of these objects can serve as a location or spot that they can use to hang their memories on.

- **STEP 3:** Now the fun part. The effectiveness of the method of loci depends a lot upon a person's imagination. This is the step where you put that imagination to work. The task your participants have now is to create an image in their head that connects a spot in their house or apartment with the item on the list. They may need a little help from you to make these images. Here are a few suggestions for the list and the locations previously mentioned:

1.  Bread—garage: Create an image in which the person sees two huge loaves of bread parked where two cars would normally be.
2.  Milk—oil burner: Imagine that the oil burner is filled with milk. It might even help if the person imagines that some milk is spilling out of the burner.

3. Peanut butter—stairs to first floor: Picture each step on the stairway covered in sticky peanut butter.

4. Broccoli—stove: You could imagine that the stove has four pots on top and each pot is filled with broccoli, or perhaps the door to the stove has been forced open and is overflowing with a pile of burnt broccoli.

5. Cereal—TV: You could imagine that the TV is on and a commercial for cereal is playing, but that's not very weird . . . and the weirder the image the better. You could imagine that bowls of cereal have been dumped on top of the TV and that soggy cereal and milk are dripping down the front of the TV.

6. Frozen pizza—dining room table: Again, you could create an easy image such as imagining that there's a plate at each spot on the table and on the plate is a slice of pizza. Or you could go for something weirder. How about imagining that the table is not rectangular but rather triangular like the shape of a pizza slice and that there's one huge slice of pizza on it?

7. Eggs—stairs to second floor: Imagine that there are cracked eggs on every step of the stairs.

8. Cat (or dog) food—bathroom at the top of the stairs: You could imagine that the bathtub is filled with cat food.

9. Toilet paper—bedroom: Try imagining that the sheets or blankets on the bed are made of toilet paper.

10. Carrots—den: Imagine that the legs to the desk are made out of carrots.

- **STEP 4:** Once your subjects understand the method of loci tell them they have 5 minutes to use the technique to memorize the items on the list. Start your stopwatch and let them go to it.

- **STEP 5:** After the 5 minutes are up, give members of group A a blank piece of paper and ask them to write down as many words as they can think of.

### GROUP B: COMPARISON GROUP

- **STEP 1:** Give this group the same list of grocery items as you gave group A and tell them that you'll give them 5 minutes to look at the list and try to memorize it. Say "go" and start your stopwatch. Of course, you won't be teaching them the method of loci, but you may find afterward that your subjects try to come up with some method on their own. A very well-known strategy is to try to make a word out of the first letters of each item in the list. Whatever list of items you come up with, make sure that the first letters of the items don't easily lend themselves to a word.

- **STEP 2:** After the 5 minutes are up give members of group B a blank piece of paper and ask them to write down as many words as they can think of.

## THE RESULTS

What you're looking for (the *dependent variable*, as scientists call it) is the number of items from the list that each person correctly recalled. Chances are the loci group recalls all or nearly all of the grocery items, whereas the comparison group recalls about 5 of them. Because of the primacy and recency effect (see the chapter titled "Your Memory Is Better Than You Think"), your comparison group will probably remember a couple from the beginning of the list and a few from the very end. That's what tends to happen when we're presented with a lot of info—we remember something from the beginning and some from the end.

Also, I'll bet your loci group members are really, really surprised at how many items they remembered. This typically happens when people learn how to use a mnemonic technique. You can take this research a step further: wait a week and then return to your group members and ask them to write down as many items from the list as they can recall. Once again, you'll probably find to everyone's surprise that the loci group remembers most if not all the items.

## WHY IT MATTERS

Your memory can be much better than you think. You might want to use the method of loci in school or at work. Many people try to remember what they learn in class by writing down terms and definitions on flashcards. This can be a good technique, but what learners are often doing is just repeating the definitions over and over again in their heads. This is not very effective as the information has nothing to "stick" to. The method of loci, on the other hand, uses familiar locations in your life as well as odd imagery. Thus, the new info "sticks" to older info and the new info is in a form (visual) that is odd enough to recall. Try using this technique the next time you have either a grocery list or important ideas from class to remember.

# GETTING WORKERS TO BE MORE PRODUCTIVE

## *WORKING HARD OR HARDLY WORKING?*

**PSYCH CONCEPT:** Motivation/Goal Setting
**NAME OF EXPERIMENT:** Assigned versus Participative Goal Setting with Educated and Uneducated Woods Workers
**ORIGINAL SCIENTIST/RESEARCH:** Gary P. Latham and Gary A. Yukl (1975)

SOCIAL

Motivating yourself and others is one of the most difficult challenges facing psychologists. You will find many so-called motivational videos on the web, and they are indeed inspiring to watch. They can also make you feel like getting up and getting to work. But the effect is usually short lasting. The videos are fun to watch, but have little impact on your daily life.

Psychologists who work in the area of industrial/organizational psychology have been working with managers in corporations for years to help them get their employees motivated. But managers are looking for more than just employees who feel "psyched up" or in a good mood. They need employees who are going to make more of a product (if the employees work in manufacturing), or make that product faster or increase their sales. If you have ever worked in a retail store—perhaps selling clothes or electronic devices—the company wants you to be able to be a good salesperson and to increase your sales from one month to the next. Other industries that need motivated employees are car sales, real estate, insurance, and fitness clubs. Obviously, showing these workers a motivational video is not going to keep them motivated to increase their sales month after month. So what strategy is one of the most effective that psychologists have developed? It's goal setting. Lots and lots of studies have been done in many different settings, and the results almost always come out the same: people who have goals may not necessarily reach their exact goal, but they will always outperform people who don't set goals.

You can demonstrate this for yourself in this rather straightforward experiment.

## THE ORIGINAL EXPERIMENT

The most famous study that established how effective goal setting can be was conducted by Gary Latham and Gary Yukl back in 1975. They were trying to solve a specific problem: how to get workers to cut down trees to increase their productivity (or, simply put, to cut down more trees). They took a group of loggers (called "sawyers" back in that day) and split them into three groups. During the eight weeks of the study, some of these sawyers were asked to set a "high, but achievable" goal to increase their productivity. Others worked with their bosses to set this high but achievable increase. A third group was not given any goals, but simply asked to "do their best" over the upcoming eight weeks. Not surprisingly to us today, the group of sawyers who set their own high but achievable goals were the ones who cut the most trees. Those who worked with their bosses to set their goals did a little less well (which shows that setting your own goals is usually best) and the group that set no particular goals but rather were just told to "do their best" showed no significant increase in productivity. This study had a big impact on how goal setting is used in just about every industry today.

## LET'S TRY IT!

You probably don't want to cut down any trees or ask your friends to do that either, so let's take a slightly different approach. In situations like this, psychologists have turned to a very useful little task: solving anagrams. As a reminder, an anagram is a word whose letters can be rearranged to create a different word. A good example is the word "east." Take a close look at the letters that make up this word. You could rearrange these letters to make the words "eats," "seat," or "teas." You can easily find lists of anagrams on the web—just search for something like "list of anagrams." You'll want to avoid words that are too short and therefore too easy to solve (like "its," which can be rearranged into "sit") but you also don't want long words like "terrain," which can be rearranged to make the word "trainer." Figuring out the word "trainer" could take some subjects a long time, and in any case it's not necessary to use difficult anagrams. What we're going to be looking for in this experiment is how many a person can solve within a certain time, so we don't want to frustrate anyone (too much).

The first thing you'll need is a list of 20 anagrams. Choose 20 words that all have the same number of letters. Four letters will probably work, though you may want to try five-letter words if you find that all your subjects are discovering the anagram solution to almost all your words. Here are some sample four-letter words you might use:

- salt (last)
- sour (ours)
- mace (came)
- near (earn)
- note (tone)
- peat (tape)
- ream (mare)
- ring (grin)
- tray (arty)
- veto (vote)

Some of the words in that list are easy and some are harder, and that's what you want—a challenging task. Once you have your 20 words you may want to do a "pilot study" by giving your words to someone who is very similar to the people you think you'll use in your study. You would want this person to be able to figure out perhaps 10–15 words during the 5 minutes. If he or she can solve all 20, you need to choose harder words. If the person solves only 1–5 of them, you need to choose easier ones.

Getting Workers to Be More Productive

Once you've got your list of words, print out sheets with the words on them and you're ready to go. Here is what you'll need for this experiment:

- 2 groups of participants
- List of 20 anagram words
- Paper and writing implements for subjects
- Stopwatch

**WHAT TO DO:**

### GROUP A

- **STEP 1:** Sit your subjects down individually. You could do this experiment in a group, but sometimes it's hard for people to not shout out the answer or talk to each other, and that would ruin your study.
- **STEP 2:** Give your subjects the piece of paper with the list of words that need to be rearranged. Give each one a pencil or pen and ask them to write the anagram to the right of the original word. It's fine if they want to doodle on the back to try out a few combinations.
- **STEP 3:** Before your subjects begin, tell them that you're going to give them 5 minutes to figure out what other word each of the words in the list could become if you rearrange the letters. Tell them you'd like them to get 17 words figured out in that time. Also, tell them that you'll let them know when 2½ minutes have passed so that they know where they stand.

### GROUP B: COMPARISON GROUP

- **STEP 1:** Follow same procedure as in group A.
- **STEP 2:** Follow same procedure as in group A.
- **STEP 3:** This time don't ask your participants to get 17 figured out in the 5 minutes. Just ask them to "do your best" in the 5 minutes. Tell them also when 2½ minutes are up.

## THE RESULTS

You should find what Latham and Yukl found: the group that was given a goal should figure out significantly more than the group without a goal. If that isn't your finding, play around with your anagrams. Remember, they should be not too easy and not too hard. The other thing you could do is to not tell group B when 2½ minutes are up. This should give you the same results as other researchers have found.

## WHY IT MATTERS

This section started by acknowledging that it's really, really hard to motivate people or even yourself. Setting goals is one strategy that seems to work in a variety of situations. Most people who want to lose weight are encouraged to set a specific goal. Losing "some weight, sometime this year" is probably not going to help. If you're a student and you're sitting down to study it would probably help if you took a minute to set out a goal for the upcoming hour. Decide how many pages of your textbook you want to read in the next hour. Make sure that you set a specific, high (but achievable) number of pages and that you check the time when you're halfway through to see how you're doing against your goal. Goal setting is one of the most useful tools psychologists can offer to those who really need to get things done.

# HOW YOU CAN IMPROVE YOUR CREATIVE ABILITY

## SOMETIMES A CIGAR CAN BE A WHOLE LOT OF THINGS

**PSYCH CONCEPT:** Functional Fixedness

**NAME OF EXPERIMENT:** The Influence of Strength of Drive on Functional Fixedness and Perceptual Recognition

**ORIGINAL SCIENTIST/RESEARCH:** Sam Glucksberg (1962)

COGNITION

We tend to think that creativity is something that some people were born with and that you're either a creative person or you're not. We think this way because we have attached the idea of creativity to artistic or musical ability. Talent in these fields is indeed hard to explain, though the ability to draw or to play instruments is far more often the result of many, many hours of practice than it is the result of "inspiration." The fact is that creativity is the ability to think outside the box—to think in ways in which most other people do not. Even that definition sounds complicated, but after you do this experiment you'll come away with a deeper understanding of what creativity is really about.

## THE ORIGINAL EXPERIMENT

It's really, really hard to measure the idea of creativity, but in 1945 psychologist Karl Duncker came up with a way to do it. His method has become very popular. Here's a description of Duncker's very simple "puzzle": suppose I gave you a box of tacks, a small candle, and a box of matches. Using only these materials, find a way to attach the candle to the wall and light it. People who have been given this problem are often stumped for quite a while. Some solutions (which aren't correct) are to tack the candle to the wall. But let's agree that these are typical-sized tacks and that they would not fit through a candle and into a wall.

The only way to solve the problem is to not see the box as merely a holder for the tacks. To solve this, you take the tacks out of the box.

Next, tack the box to the wall. Then light the candle and melt a little of the wax onto the center of the bottom of the box. Then blow out the candle and stick it into this wax so that it is standing straight up. Then you can relight the candle.

You can see why in order to solve the problem you have to overcome functional fixedness. You have to see the box as not just a box that can hold tacks, but as a box that could also serve as a way to hold up the candle.

Sam Glucksberg later created an experiment using Duncker's idea, and that's the one we'll replicate here. It's pretty straightforward: present the "candle problem" to one group of subjects as it has just been described and then for another group, remove the tacks from the box and just put them separately in front of the subjects. Those subjects are able to solve the problem quite quickly.

## LET'S TRY IT!

This is not a difficult experiment to replicate. You could do pretty much what Glucksberg did. You'll need these items:

- 2 groups of participants
- 4–5 small boxes made out of paper or cardboard
- 10–12 tacks
- 12 (6-inch-long) candles
- Matchboxes containing matches
- Stopwatch

## WHAT TO DO:

### *GROUP A*

- **STEP 1:** Sit your subjects down at a table and have the materials laid out in front of them—but make sure that the tacks are inside the box.
- **STEP 2:** Tell them that you're going to ask them a question about these materials, and that they can pick them up if they wish. Have a stopwatch ready. If they ask about the stopwatch, feel free to tell them that you're going to write down how many minutes it takes them to come up with a solution to a problem you're going to pose to them but that there's no reason to rush—you just want to collect accurate data with the stopwatch.
- **STEP 3:** When they're ready ask them this question: "Using only the materials you see here, how would you attach the candle to a wall and light it?" They may repeat the question out loud, which is okay, but if they ask any further questions try not to give anything away. Just stick to this key question.
- **STEP 4:** Let them know they can begin and start your stopwatch as unobtrusively as you can (perhaps under the table or by your side).
- **STEP 5:** There is only one solution (though I've heard students come up with some pretty unusual ones over the years), and that involves lighting the candle with the matches, taking the tacks out of the box, melting a little wax into the box so you can stick the bottom of the candle onto the wax and then tacking the box and candle to the wall. When that solution is arrived at, stop your watch and record the time.

### *GROUP B*

- **STEP 1:** As with group A, you'll sit your subjects down at a table and have the materials laid out in front of them. However, this time you'll make sure that the tacks are not inside the box.

How You Can Improve Your Creative Ability

- **STEP 2:** As in group A tell them that you're going to ask them a question about these materials, and that they can pick them up if they wish. Have a stopwatch ready.
- **STEP 3:** When they're ready ask them this question: "Using only the materials you see here, how would you attach the candle to a wall and light it?" As in group A these participants may repeat the question out loud, but if they ask any further questions try not to give anything away.
- **STEP 4:** Let them know they can begin and start your stopwatch.
- **STEP 5:** When the correct solution is reached, stop the watch and record the results.

## THE RESULTS

What you should find is that the participants in group B will come up with the solution (or one that is very near to it) much faster than the participants in group A. By taking the tacks out of the box you have allowed your participants to see the box as a container for just about anything and not just for the tacks. It's pretty amazing what such a small change can do to a person's mindset.

## WHY IT MATTERS

Creativity, or the ability not to get stuck in functional fixedness, is a skill that you can develop and that is very much in need in the workplace. Employees quite often think creatively but don't identify it as such. However, the only way to come up with new products to sell in stores is to look at what exists and think of it in a different way. The companies of tomorrow will depend on the ability of its employees to do this kind of thinking. So start challenging yourself: look at ordinary objects and imagine what else they could be used for.

# MENTAL SETS CAN LIMIT YOU INTO ONE WAY OF THINKING

## HOW TO GET UNSTUCK

**PSYCH CONCEPT:** Mental Set

**NAME OF EXPERIMENT:** Classroom Experiments on Mental Set

**ORIGINAL SCIENTIST/RESEARCH:** Abraham S. Luchins (1946)

COGNITION

Have you ever heard the expression, "If all you have is a hammer, everything becomes a nail"? It can be applied to a lot of different situations, but what we're interested in is that sometimes we all approach new problems with the same old "mindset." That is, we apply old ways of thinking to new problems that have absolutely nothing to do with that old way. If you're working on a problem—whether a math problem in school or even a problem with your car—and you can't figure out how to solve it, you have probably said to yourself, "I'm just stuck." Luchins's experiment, now over seventy years old, was one of the first to demonstrate how we can get into a mental set and what we can do to get out of it. Let's dive in.

## THE ORIGINAL EXPERIMENT

Since mental sets often happen with math problems, Luchins used these kinds of problems to demonstrate the essential idea of a mental set. He used two groups of students in his study. One group was given problems to solve like this one:

There is an empty 29-quart jar and an empty 3-quart jar as well as a large body of water from which you may draw and into which you may pour water; e.g. a well. You are to obtain exactly 20 quarts of water.

Sounds like one of those math problems you hated in high school. This one is actually not that hard to solve. Here's how Luchins described the solution to subjects if they didn't figure it out:

Fill the 29-quart jar. Pour 3 quarts from it into the smaller jar, thus leaving 26 quarts in the large container. Empty the 3-quart jar and fill it once again. Now 23 quarts remain in the large jar. Again fill the 3-quart jar and the required 20 quarts are in the large container.

Okay, you say, so where's the psychology in this? So here's what Luchins did next: he gave one group of subjects nine more problems. The first five problems used these same hypothetical jars of water and the solution to each of these problems was to do essentially the same thing you did the first time—fill up the big container and then pour water out of it into the smaller container until you had the requested amount.

The tricky part comes when subjects reached question numbers 7, 8, and 9. Without going into detail, problems 7 and 8 could be solved by the approach just described, but there was also a much simpler way to solve them. Question 9 could not be solved using the same approach as the first few described. To solve it you had to come up with a completely different method.

Before explaining what happened it's important to know that Luchins's second group, group B, was given problems 7, 8, and 9 but they were not given the first 5 problems.

So what happened? The group that was given the first 5 problems to solve and repeatedly used the same approach (that of filling the big jar with water and then pouring out water into the smaller jars) had a very hard time figuring out questions 7 and 8—even though those two

Mental Sets Can Limit You Into One Way of Thinking

questions were easier than the ones they had already solved! And this group also took a long time figuring out question 9 because it required a completely different approach from the earlier problems. What happened was that the subjects got "stuck" in a mental set. They applied what worked in an old problem to solving a new one.

Members of group B were not provided with an opportunity to get stuck, and they solved questions 7, 8, and 9 (which were just questions 1, 2, and 3 for them) much quicker than group A.

## LET'S TRY IT!

We can replicate this "mental set" phenomenon in a way that's a little more fun than Luchins's approach. We'll use ambiguous images. Have you seen the image that looks either like an old woman or a young woman? There are also images that look like they could be a drawing of either a duck or a rabbit, and even the vase/faces black-and-white image that some people use to represent the field of psychology. Here's a link to the Wikipedia page where you can see some of these images: https://en.wikipedia.org/wiki/Ambiguous_image. And here is the old woman/young woman image that you could use in this experiment:

What we'll do is "set up" one group of people to be inclined to see this image as an old woman and set up another group to see it as a young woman. Here is what you will need:

- 2 groups of participants
- 10 images of young women, printed about the same size (say 5" × 7")
- Image of old woman/young woman (11th image)

- 10 images of old women, printed about the same size (say 5" × 7")

## WHAT TO DO:

### GROUP A

- **STEP 1:** Sit your subjects down and tell them that you're going to show them 10 images and then ask them what they think the 11th image is a picture of.
- **STEP 2:** When they're ready, simply place the 10 images of young women one at a time in front of your subjects. Wait about 5 seconds between each image.
- **STEP 3:** Before you lay down the last image of the old woman/ young woman, tell your subjects that you're going to put down an image that might be unclear at first, but that they should take a look at it and take a guess as to what they think it's a picture of.

### GROUP B

- **STEP 1:** Sit your subjects down and tell them that you're going to show them 10 images and then ask them what they think the 11th image is a picture of.
- **STEP 2:** When they're ready, simply place the 10 images of old women one at a time in front of your subjects. Wait about 5 seconds between each image.
- **STEP 3:** Before you lay down the last image of the old woman/ young woman, tell your subjects that you're going to put down an image that might be unclear at first, but that they should take a look at it and take a guess as to what they think it's a picture of.

## THE RESULTS

The repeated images of the young woman or the old woman should put your subjects into a mental set. You should find that those who saw pictures of older women identified the ambiguous image as an older woman, and vice versa.

## WHY IT MATTERS

If you haven't yet had this "I'm stuck" experience in life—feeling that you just can't figure out how to solve a problem—you will at some point. You've probably been looking at the problem in the same way repeatedly, as your subjects did in this experiment. So how do you "break" the mental set? Probably the best way is to take a walk. No doubt you've also heard someone say that they have to "sleep on it." That's also good advice. When you get away from the problem for a while your brain is "loosened up" a bit and you're able to come back and look at it again with a different mindset.

# NOTICING A FACE IN THE CROWD

## *I NEVER FORGET A FACE*

**PSYCH CONCEPT:** Identifying Emotions

**NAME OF EXPERIMENT:** Constants Across Cultures in the Face and Emotion

**ORIGINAL SCIENTIST/RESEARCH:** Paul Ekman and Wallace V. Friesen (1971)

**NAME OF REPLICATION/EXTENSION:** Finding the Face in the Crowd: An Anger Superiority Effect

**REPLICATION SCIENTIST/RESEARCH:** Christine H. Hansen and Ranald D. Hansen (1988)

EMOTIONS

Have you ever wondered whether people around the world recognize an angry face when they see it? How about a happy face? Those emotions are perhaps easy to pick out, but how about a frown? A sad face? A scared face? Maybe you've noticed when a child of, say, five or six years old displays a look of confusion on his face? So the question for psychologists has been how we learn to make these faces and whether people in other cultures change their facial expressions in the same way in order to communicate the same emotion. Researchers Ekman and Friesen found some pretty amazing things when they looked at this question. In this section we're going to focus on the emotions of happiness and anger.

## THE ORIGINAL EXPERIMENT

Ekman and Friesen believed that emotional expression was universal—that everyone, no matter where they live, recognizes the same facial expression as happy or sad, angry or disgusted. To prove his point they needed a group of people who had very limited contact with the rest of the world. They wanted people who had not been exposed to television or movies. They found these people in the Southeast Highlands of New Guinea. They were a group of people called the Fore. The Fore had not had any exposure to any facial expressions other than from the faces of their own people. Ekman and Friesen went into the villages ready to give their subjects a simple task: the translator read a brief description of a person who was in a specific mood and the researchers showed the villagers pictures of three faces. Only one of those faces showed the expression that matched the person's mood.

Here's an example: one description (often just a sentence) was about a child who just lost his (or her) mother and he (or she) felt very sad. After being read this sentence the participant was then shown three pictures of people showing different expressions—one of which of course was a sad expression. People from this study correctly identified the expression most of the time (80–90 percent). Sadness and anger were the most easily recognized expressions. The results from the Fore people were not significantly different from people who took this same test but who were from Western cultures. So apparently, there is a certain universality when it comes to facial expressions. No matter where you're brought up, we all make the same expressions.

## LET'S TRY IT!

Now, I'm going to guess that you don't have access to a group of people who have never been exposed to Western culture. How, then, might you look into this facial expression topic? There is a way. Notice that anger was an expression that was correctly identified by people from many cultures. Researchers Hansen and Hansen think the reason is that an angry face is something you really have to pay attention to. People in a state of anger are a potential threat to your survival. People with happy faces are probably not going to be a cause for concern. So from an evolutionary perspective it's not surprising that people from different cultures are highly accurate in identifying angry faces. That skill is important for survival.

So Hansen and Hansen did an interesting experiment that you can do yourself. They showed subjects pictures of small crowds of people. In some of these pictures, most of the people were showing happy faces; in others, most of them were displaying angry faces—*most*, but not all. Inside the pictures of happy people there was one person who was angry. Inside the pictures of angry people there was one person who was happy. Subjects were shown a bunch of such photos and asked to see if they could find someone whose facial expression was not like the rest of the crowd.

What did they find? Their subjects were quicker to find the angry face in the happy crowd than they were to find the happy face in an angry crowd. Again—finding angry faces is a very important skill for humans to have, and apparently we are born with an inclination to readily identify angry people.

This study isn't hard to replicate, but as you may have guessed, you're going to need some friends and a few other things:

- About 30 people for the crowd photos
- Camera (or use your smartphone camera)
- 2 groups of participants (not members of the crowd)
- Stopwatch
- Paper and pencil (to record responses on)

**WHAT TO DO:**

### *GROUP A: ANGRY FACE IN HAPPY CROWD*
- **STEP 1:** Create your 10 crowd photos. Get about 30 people together and mix and match them for every photo you take (you'll want 9 people minimum in each photo but more is fine). Each time before you take a photo ask everybody except one person to make

a happy face. You ask one person to make an angry face, making sure that person does not go overboard and make a really, really angry face (that would make the participants' task too easy). Make sure it's a different person making the angry face in each picture. To make sure it doesn't look like you're using the same people for each photo you could ask members of the group to borrow pieces of clothing from each other or wear a jacket in one photo but not the other. And of course, if you've got 30 people to choose from, you're not using the same 9 people each time. After you've got your photos you're ready to test out this idea on your subjects (none of whom can come from the group of people you used for your photos).

- **STEP 2:** Sit your subjects down and have your stopwatch ready. Tell each person that you're going to show them 10 photos and that you'd like them to look at them and pick out someone who they think has a facial expression different from everybody else. Don't tell them that this person has an angry face. They can also say "No" if they don't think there is such a person.

- **STEP 3:** Give them the first photo and start your stopwatch. Stop it when they select a person. Mark down the results: how long it took them to find the person with the angry face. If they identify the wrong person or can't find anyone whose face is "different," mark this down as an error.

### GROUP B: HAPPY FACE IN ANGRY CROWD

- **STEP 1:** Create your 10 crowd photos the same way you did for group A. You can even use the same people. Just make sure that one person shows a happy face (not overly happy) while the others are angry. When you've got your 10 photos you're ready to run your participant group.

- **STEP 2:** Sit your subjects down and have your stopwatch ready. Tell each person that you're going to show them 10 photos and that you'd like them to look at them and pick out someone who they think has a facial expression different from everybody else. Don't tell them that this person has a happy face. They can also say "No" if they don't think there is such a person.

- **STEP 3:** Give them the first photo and start your stopwatch. Stop it when they select a person. Mark down the results: how long it took them to find the person with the happy face. If they identify the wrong person or can't find anyone whose face is "different," mark this down as an error.

## THE RESULTS

We've simplified Hansen and Hansen's study a bit, but hopefully you'll find the same thing they did: times were faster when the angry person was in a group of happy people. You might also find that there were more errors in group B (happy person in an angry crowd). We as humans are just more attuned to angry faces than happy ones.

## WHY IT MATTERS

This is one of the many studies that support the subfield of evolutionary psychology. Psychologists have found that many behaviors—even how we choose our romantic partners—can be explained by aspects of evolution theory. In this case we find that "picking out a face in the crowd" might be easier than you think—if that face looks like it's going to threaten your life!

# HOW TO THINK MORE POSITIVELY ABOUT LIFE

## *SING YOUR PROBLEMS AWAY*

**PSYCH CONCEPT:** Cognitive Therapy/Cognitive Defusion

**NAME OF EXPERIMENT:** Using Brief Cognitive Restructuring and Cognitive Defusion Techniques to Cope with Negative Thoughts

**ORIGINAL SCIENTIST/RESEARCH:** Andreas Larsson, Nic Hooper, Lisa A. Osborne, Paul Bennett, and Louise McHugh (2015)

COGNITION

Many people think that if they go to see a psychologist they will have to talk about their past. This is not always the case. After you sit down and talk to a therapist about what you're experiencing and what you'd like to get out of therapy, there are number of very different approaches that a therapist could take to try to help you with whatever you're troubled by. This may have nothing to do with exploring your childhood.

We all "talk to ourselves" quietly in our heads. We think about how the day went or what someone said to us and what it means. Well, cognitive psychologists are interested in what you say to yourself throughout the day. Some of us have a tendency to interpret what happens to us in a negative way. When things don't go well we might say something to ourselves like, "I can't do anything right," or "How stupid could I be?" If you have a tendency to do that, a therapist might work with you to try to change that negative thought pattern. This process is more complex than just repeating some positive statement over and over again—that's just pop psychology. Real psychologists are looking for patterns in your thinking, and they're going to help clients change these patterns.

One new approach, believe it or not, is to use a few popular cell phone games to help you achieve a more positive outlook. How can you use such games to help people feel better about themselves? Let's find out.

## THE ORIGINAL EXPERIMENT

Andreas Larsson and his colleagues did a study in which groups of people wrote down some of negative thoughts that occurred to them during the day and then the researchers had them use one of two techniques to combat these negative thoughts: cognitive restructuring or cognitive defusion. Sounds complicated but it's not.

*Cognitive restructuring* (or "rebuilding") involves writing your thought down and looking at how rational the thought is. For example, suppose you sometimes have the thought that you "can't do anything right." A psychologist would call that kind of thought an overgeneralization. In other words, you may have messed one thing up, but is it really the case that you can't do "anything" right? You probably do a lot of things right. So the goal here is to not have you generalize from one bad experience to your whole life. So you might be asked to restructure that thought into something more realistic like "Okay, I didn't do well on this, but it's not going to affect the rest of my life." Doing this gives you a little distance from that negative thought.

But there's another way to give you distance from your thoughts and to help you realize that the thought is unrealistic. And that's to sing it. Or to have Bugs Bunny speak your thoughts. Yes, you heard right. What if you were asked to sing this line: "I can't do anything right"? After a few minutes of singing this (or hearing Bugs Bunny say it) you would begin to think of it as kind of funny rather than sad. This is known as *cognitive defusion*. There are several of these "defusion" techniques but their goal is the same: to help you get some "distance" from your thoughts.

So maybe we can get you to think less negatively if we make some of your thoughts sound silly—even to you. Let's see if we can replicate what Larsson did.

Larsson brought participants into a lab and asked them to write down thoughts they have had about themselves that had these qualities: "extremely negative," "extremely uncomfortable," and also "extremely believable." After this, they were asked to rate each thought on a scale of 1–5. Over a five-day period participants used either restructuring or defusion techniques to manage the negative thoughts. Daily questionnaires assessed how the participants felt the negative thoughts affected them. Larsson found that defusion lowered the believability of the negative thoughts and increased comfort and willingness to have the thought more so than cognitive restructuring techniques.

## LET'S TRY IT!

Go ahead and download one of those "voice changing" apps. A popular one is called "Songify," but you'll find many others if you do a web search on the term "voice changing apps." Many people are timid about singing in front of anyone, so we'll make this easier for them by using an app that they can talk into and have the app turn what they said into a funny voice. Therapists who use the defusion technique use these voice changing apps.

Larsson's subjects were people who actually were feeling down, but we won't ask your friends to reveal their negative thoughts or feelings, because that's quite personal. Instead we'll give them some typical negative statements that people say to themselves and ask how uncomfortable they think the statement would make another person feel. Like Larsson, we'll compare how effective it is to try to "restructure" that negative thought versus the effect of changing the thought into something that just sounds silly.

So here's what you'll need:

- 2 groups of participants
- Smartphone with a voice changing app. Make sure you're familiar with how the app works and that the app can change a simple statement into a funny voice (a rabbit, a robot, a zombie, etc.).
- Piece of paper with these 3 statements printed on the front and the back: I make a mess of everything; No one will ever love me; I am stupid. Below each statement put a short blank line.

## WHAT TO DO:

### GROUP A: RESTRUCTURING GROUP

- **STEP 1:** Sit your subjects down one by one and show them the statements on one side of the page. Tell them that these are things that some people sometimes say to themselves. Ask them to pick a number between 1 and 20 and rate the statement as to how uncomfortable that statement would probably make someone feel if they said that to themselves.

- **STEP 2:** When they're done have a little talk with them about how irrational the statements are. The first one is an example of overgeneralization—does anyone really make a mess of absolutely everything they do? The second is an example of black-and-white thinking—is it true that absolutely no one will ever love the person? The third is labeling—we may all do some things that are not so smart at the time but are we actually stupid?

- **STEP 3:** After you have this talk turn the paper over and ask them to rate the sentences again from 1–20. You'll probably find that they give the statements a slightly lower rating.

### GROUP B: DEFUSION GROUP

- **STEP 1:** Repeat step 1 from group A. (Show the statements and ask the participants to rate their levels on comfort.)

- **STEP 2:** Do NOT have the conversation with this group about the irrationality of the statements. Instead, after they have rated the statements on one side of the paper, get out your voice changing app. Have them record themselves saying each statement one at a time into your app. Then change the recording of their voice into some voice that is funny (or have Songify make them sound like they just sang it).
- **STEP 3:** Have participants listen to the recording a couple of times.
- **STEP 4:** Do this same procedure with the other two statements. Then turn the paper over and ask them to rate the statements again from 1–20.

## THE RESULTS

You'll probably find that the defusion group changed their ratings even more than the restructuring group. Even if they changed their ratings to the more "comfortable" side of the scale only a little bit, this shows that they got a little psychological "distance" from these negative thoughts, and that's good.

## WHY IT MATTERS

It's important for us all to listen to the things we say to ourselves and to make sure that what we say is realistic. Sometimes what we say to ourselves just couldn't be true and it's only going to make us feel bad if we give those thoughts a lot of weight. What you found out in this experiment is that there are different ways to get that distance—either by thinking more carefully about what you actually said and then saying it in a different way (restructuring) or just by realizing how ridiculous the statement is when you hear it in a funny voice (defusion).

# HOW PSYCHIATRIC LABELS AFFECT HOW WE SEE PEOPLE

## STICKS AND STONES MAY NOT BREAK MY BONES, BUT LABELS MAY INCARCERATE ME

**PSYCH CONCEPT:** Labeling and Mental Illness

**NAME OF EXPERIMENT:** On Being Sane in Insane Places

**ORIGINAL SCIENTIST/RESEARCH:** David L. Rosenhan (1974)

**NAME OF REPLICATION/EXTENSION:** The Power of Language and Labels: "The Mentally Ill" versus "People with Mental Illnesses"

**REPLICATION SCIENTIST/RESEARCH:** Darcy Haag Granello and Todd A. Gibbs (2016)

COGNITION

In one of psychology's most famous studies, the lead researcher, one of his students, and several of his friends deliberately went to a psychiatric hospital and tried to get themselves admitted. They wanted to see if it would be easy or hard to do. They also wondered what would happen if, after getting admitted, they then acted completely normally. Would the staff recognize that a mistake had been made? Could they distinguish "odd" behavior from "normal" behavior? And they wondered how long it would take before they would be released.

All these questions are about the effects of labeling. Once we give someone a label, such as "depressed" or "schizophrenic," are we then able to see that person in any other way? What if a depressed person is able to overcome depression—will she now be seen as "normal" or will she be seen as "a formerly depressed person"? How powerful are labels in terms of how we see people?

## THE ORIGINAL EXPERIMENT

Rosenhan and his seven associates all agreed before they went to the psychiatric hospital that they would all say the same things to the admissions person: that they were hearing voices that said "empty," "hollow," and "thud." After they were interviewed, all of them were admitted. Some were given a diagnosis of schizophrenia and one with manic-depression (what today we call bipolar disorder). After admission, they all acted normally. They took notes every day on their experience. As it turned out, they were held in the hospitals anywhere from one week to almost two months before being released. As for their note taking—it appeared by some staff to be a compulsive behavior. Once they were released, their psychiatric condition was considered by the hospitals to be "in remission."

This study gave the psychological community serious concerns about the effects of labeling. Psychiatric labels are considered important because they help mental health workers have a better understanding of what a person is suffering from and what medications or therapies are best to treat that condition. Think about it: you probably wouldn't trust a medical doctor who didn't have a name for your condition. However, the problem with labels is that they can "stick" and it can be hard to then think of a person as a human being and not a label. In the same way that patients with medical conditions, such as appendicitis, can be considered healthy after their treatment, we need to be aware that just because we label someone with a psychological disorder doesn't mean that he can't make significant enough progress to be considered free of the problem.

Let's find out how powerful labels can be in this experiment, in which we make one tiny change in a job applicant's self-description.

# LET'S TRY IT!

We'll use a simple, often used data-gathering technique that sheds light on how our looks, race, ethnicity, and even facial expression affects people's perception of our appropriateness for a hypothetical job. Facts about a person such as their race or looks shouldn't have anything to do with how qualified we think they are for a job, but these qualities do in fact play a role. Here is what you'll need:

- 2 groups of participants
- 2 descriptions of hypothetical applicant (see following)

All you'll need to carry out this experiment is to tell your participants that you want to know how successful they think this person will be at a job. We'll use a job title that perhaps people are not that familiar with: Marketing Manager.

## WHAT TO DO:

### GROUP A
- **STEP 1:** You can make up a description of a job applicant, but here's one as a sample. Notice in this description that Janet is a "mentally ill" person:

Janet is an outgoing person in her twenties. She graduated from college with a degree in marketing. While in college she was a member of the school's marketing club, for which she served as the key fundraiser. She headed up many fundraising activities during that time. She also attended two marketing conferences to learn as much as she could about the field. In high school she received excellent grades and was a competitive swimmer on the school's swim team. Her parents divorced when she was twelve and for a while she was a bit of a "loner." She was taken to a counselor and spent the next year in therapy to help her deal with depression. Afterward she was better able to deal with home and school life and though she is a mentally ill person, she did quite well in college and is enthusiastic about a career in marketing and sales. She just took an apartment in Boston and is beginning her job search with optimism.

- **STEP 2:** Put the job title of Marketing Manager at the top of the page and print out a piece of paper with your description.
- **STEP 3:** Working with one subject at a time, ask your subject to read the description and give Janet a number from 1–10 to indicate how successful she is likely to be at the job (1 being not at all successful and 10 being very successful). If your subject says that he doesn't feel like he can make an accurate decision without more information or without meeting "Janet," just ask him to go with a gut feeling and choose a number.
- **STEP 4:** After the participant gives you a number, thank him and then move on to your next subject.

### *GROUP B*

- **STEP 1:** Group B is also given a description of "Janet" but as you'll see in this sample, she is described slightly differently: she is "a person with a mental illness."

Janet is an outgoing person in her twenties. She graduated from college with a degree in marketing. While in college she was a member of the school's marketing club, for which she served as the key fundraiser. She headed up many fundraising activities during that time. She also attended two marketing conferences to learn as much as she could about the field. In high school she received excellent grades and was a competitive swimmer on the school's swim team. Her parents divorced when she was twelve and for a while she was a bit of a "loner." She was taken to a counselor and spent the next year in therapy to help her deal with depression. Afterward she was better able to deal with home and school life and though she is a person with a mental illness, she did quite well in college and is enthusiastic about a career in marketing and sales. She just took an apartment in Boston and is beginning her job search with optimism.

- **STEP 2:** Working with one subject at a time, ask your subject to read the description and give Janet a number from 1–10 to indicate how successful she is likely to be at the job (1 being not at all successful and 10 being very successful).
- **STEP 3:** After the participant gives you a number, thank him and then move on to your next subject.

## THE RESULTS

In an attempt to deal with the negative effects of labeling, mental health workers are suggesting that the simple act of saying that a person "has a mental illness" instead of saying they "are mentally ill" will have an effect on how that person is viewed by others. You will probably see that when Janet is described as "a mentally ill person" your subjects rated her slightly lower than when she was a "person with a mental illness."

## WHY IT MATTERS

Unlike the experience of having appendicitis or the flu, when people have a psychological problem and they receive some kind of therapy society tends to not consider them "cured" afterward, even if they're not acting any differently from anyone else. This may be because mental illnesses are not something you can see. It's easier for us to understand a problem when we can see it. With mental illnesses, we just can't easily tell if a person has overcome her challenge. Also, we have a tendency to see mental illness as an either/or kind of thing: you're either "normal" or you're "ill." But that's not the case. We all have troubles at different times in our lives. Sometimes our reactions to those troubles are extreme, and sometimes they're mild. Mental illness isn't an either/or, and it's important that we not stigmatize ourselves or others because of treatment by a mental health professional.

# THE DESIGN OF EVERYDAY THINGS

## *WATCH OUT FOR THAT HOT STOVE!*

**PSYCH CONCEPT:** Human Factors/Natural Mapping
**NAME OF EXPERIMENT:** The Design of Everyday Things
**ORIGINAL SCIENTIST/RESEARCH:** Donald Norman (2002)

COGNITION

Did you ever visit a webpage and get confused as to where to click? That's a poorly designed website. Here's the flip side: a website that was so well designed that you found yourself following a set of "Click Here" buttons and then before you know it you have purchased something. That's a well-designed site (at least from the perspective of the site's owner!). Believe it or not, there's a good bit of psychology involved in designing things you interact with every day. Apple Inc. has become quite successful in part because the company designs products that seem "intuitive." You know how to work with them usually without having to refer to a manual.

We're going to do a little experiment that will show you just how quickly—and how slowly—it can take someone to operate something as ordinary as a stovetop when it has been poorly designed. What do psychologists and stovetops have to do with one another? You'd be surprised.

## THE ORIGINAL EXPERIMENT

Almost every product you buy has been subjected to some form of experiment. Large companies employ experimental psychologists to see what people actually do when they interact with a product. In this study we'll look at the design of stove burners and the knobs that control them. Typically, stove knobs are just lined up across the front of the stove. That's an easy way to design a stove, but the problem is that the burners are not lined up side by side on a stove—they are lined up with one row behind the other. So what researchers did was to present people with stoves designed in the usual way (below left). And stoves designed in a more "natural" way—that is, the knobs are placed in the same pattern as the burners (below, right).

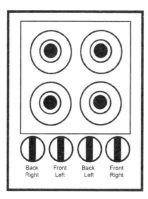
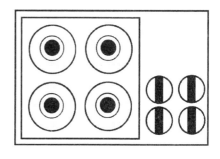

The experiment is pretty straightforward: stand people in front of the stove and ask them to turn on a specific burner. This is usually videotaped and afterward researchers record the amount of time (usually hundredths of seconds) for the person to figure out which knob controls which burner. The goal is to make that time as short as possible.

## LET'S TRY IT!

You can replicate this study in a very straightforward way. First, you need images of the two stovetops that Donald Norman examined in his research. The images are actually quite easy to find. You could go to a local store that sells stoves. You'll find some that are poorly designed, as in the first image, and some that have a more "natural" mapping. Or you could do a web search on the terms "natural mapping stove top." You'll see the two stovetops previously shown as well as other stovetops with even more burner and knob configurations. Print out a picture of the "good" stovetop and the "bad" stovetop on separate pieces of paper. Here's what you'll need for the experiment:

- 2 groups of participants
- Photo of well-designed or "natural"-designed stovetop
- Photo of "bad" stovetop design
- Pencil
- Stopwatch

**WHAT TO DO:**

*GROUP A*
- **STEP 1:** Set your stopwatch to 0. Have your "good" stovetop image turned upside down so your subjects can't see it, and have your pencil ready.
- **STEP 2:** Sit your subjects down at a table individually and tell them that you're going to show them a drawing of a stovetop with burners and knobs. You're going to point to a specific knob and ask them to point to which burner that knob controls. Make sure you answer any questions before you begin.
- **STEP 3:** When they say they're ready, turn the paper over, point to the knob on the bottom left (you can say, "That one"), and start your stopwatch. It won't take long for them to point to the correct burner. In fact, they may feel that the task was deceptively easy and wonder what you're up to. You can explain what you're doing by showing them the "good" stovetop drawing. Just make sure they don't tell anyone else what you're doing.
- **STEP 4:** Write down their time (probably just a second or two, so make sure you write down the tenths of a second as well) and write an X if they choose the wrong one or a check if the choose correctly.

## GROUP B

- **STEP 1:** Set your stopwatch to 0. This time have your "bad" stovetop image turned upside down so your subjects can't see it, and have your pencil ready.
- **STEP 2:** Sit your subjects down at a table individually and tell them that you're going to show them a drawing of a stovetop with burners and knobs. You're going to point to a specific knob and ask them to point to which burner that knob controls. Make sure you answer any questions before you begin.
- **STEP 3:** When they say they're ready, turn the paper over, point to the knob on the left (you can say, "That one"), and start your stopwatch.
- **STEP 4:** I think you'll be surprised at how confused they look when they examine the image. They'll probably say something like "umm . . ." before they figure out which burner to point to. Write down the time from your stopwatch, and if they point to the wrong burner write down an X instead of a checkmark.

## THE RESULTS

No doubt you'll find that your subjects in group B take longer to choose a burner, and there may even be mistakes in this group. It would be surprising if you had any mistakes from subjects who looked at the "natural" stovetop design.

## WHY IT MATTERS

Obviously it's important that companies design household products—especially ones that emit heat or flame—in such a way that they can be easily and correctly operated. But picture the cockpit of an airplane. There are hundreds of dials and lots of switches. It's overwhelming. While it might be a little annoying to have to take a few extra seconds to figure out which knob controls which burner on your stovetop, consider the consequences if a pilot takes too long to make a decision—or makes the wrong one—when flying an airplane. Lives are at stake. Think of this the next time you take an airplane flight. A psychologist (often called a human factors psychologist) was probably involved in the design of the cockpit.

# BEAUTY IS APPARENTLY NOT JUST IN THE EYE OF THE BEHOLDER

## *HEY GOOD LOOKIN'!*

**PSYCH CONCEPT:** Interpersonal Attraction

**NAME OF EXPERIMENT:** What Is Beautiful Is Good

**ORIGINAL SCIENTIST/RESEARCH:** Karen Dion, Ellen Berscheid, and Elaine Walster (1972)

SOCIAL

It's interesting that physical beauty is recognized by people across cultures. Your tendency to recognize someone as attractive can even be reduced to a mathematical formula. We find that when a person's body proportions meet specific ratios they tend to be seen as attractive by many people. There also seems to be a kind of halo around beautiful people. That is, we often assume that a beautiful person has other desirable qualities, like honesty and helpfulness. This was first investigated by Karen Dion, Ellen Berscheid, and Elaine Walster in the early 1970s.

## THE ORIGINAL EXPERIMENT

Dion and her colleagues gathered 100 yearbook photos, showed them to college students, and asked them to rate each person's attractiveness. The only photos used for the study were those given ratings of very high (attractive people), ordinary (average attractiveness), or low (unattractive people). The researchers then had another group of students look at this subset of photos that had been selected. That group was asked about other qualities the people in the photos might have, such as trustworthiness, kindness, altruism, and warmth. Sure enough, the attractive people were thought to have all kinds of positive qualities. Let's see how we can put this to the test.

## LET'S TRY IT!

To reproduce the key findings of this study you will need a photo of an attractive person, an average-looking person, and an unattractive person. Photos of people from the shoulders up is fine. It's best to look for pictures of people who are not well known. You can find such photos through a web search. Of course, don't ask your friends to pose for you. Nobody wants to find out that you're putting them in the "average" or "unattractive" category. The photo of the attractive person shouldn't be too glamorous. Also, your picture of the unattractive person shouldn't be someone who has obvious facial scars or other deformities. You don't want your subjects to figure out what you're up to.

Here are the materials you'll need:

- 20 participants
- Photo of attractive person
- Photo of average-looking person
- Photo of unattractive person
- 3 envelopes, each large enough to hold a photo
- 4 pieces of paper will be needed for each individual participant (The total number of pieces of paper then will depend on the total number of participants)
- Writing implements for participants

### WHAT TO DO:

- **STEP 1:** Take your three photographs and label each below the person's face: "Person 1" (average attractiveness), "Person 2" (unattractive), and "Person 3" (attractive). Print out the photos and place each photo in its own envelope.

- **STEP 2:** Put the questions you're going to ask your subjects on three separate pieces of paper. Let's use some of the same personality characteristics the authors used. Here are six traits the researchers used, along with a rating scale of 1 to 10:

Dull   **1 2 3 4 5 6 7 8 9 10**   Exciting

Cold   **1 2 3 4 5 6 7 8 9 10**   Warm

Uninteresting   **1 2 3 4 5 6 7 8 9 10**   Interesting

Unsophisticated   **1 2 3 4 5 6 7 8 9 10**   Sophisticated

Insincere   **1 2 3 4 5 6 7 8 9 10**   Sincere

Not Very Intelligent   **1 2 3 4 5 6 7 8 9 10**   Very Intelligent

So now you have three pieces of paper, titled Person 1, Person 2, and Person 3, and each piece has the six questions listed.

- **STEP 3:** On a fourth sheet of paper you'll put three questions similar to the ones used by the researchers to find out if attractive people are seen as the ones who would lead more fulfilling lives. The questions are:

1. Which person is most likely of the three to get divorced?
2. Which person will probably be the best parent?
3. Which person is most likely to be the most fulfilled in their career?

- **STEP 4:** Have your subjects take a photo out of an envelope, look at the person in the photo, and circle a number for each of the six traits.

- **STEP 5:** After they have done this for all three photos, one at a time, ask the three questions listed in step 3 and write down the number of the person they chose next to each question.

## THE RESULTS

You should find that a group of twenty people is enough to get results similar to the original study. Calculate an average score for the personality traits for each photo by adding up the circled numbers for each trait and dividing by the number of subjects in your study. You'll probably find that the photo of the attractive person got higher scores than the photos of the other two people for exciting, warm, interesting, sophisticated, sincere, and very intelligent. You'll probably also find that the attractive person is less likely to be chosen to get a divorce and more likely to be chosen to be the best parent and to have the most fulfilling career.

## WHY IT MATTERS

It's hard to escape the fact that we live in a society that is obsessed with beauty. As this study and many others show, beautiful people are assumed to have many other wonderful qualities. Curiously, there is one instance, at least, in which being very attractive could be a disadvantage: that's if you use your good looks to help you commit crimes. One study showed that if a photo of a man is shown along with a description of how this man swindled older women out of their money by pretending to be in love with them, the man was given a longer jail sentence if he was handsome. So being beautiful is great—just don't use your looks to take advantage of others.

# HOW ROLES CAN AFFECT US AT A DEEP LEVEL

## ARE YOU THE ROLE YOU PLAY?

**PSYCH CONCEPT:** Social Roles

**NAME OF EXPERIMENT:** A Study of Prisoners and Guards in a Simulated Prison

**ORIGINAL SCIENTIST/RESEARCH:** Craig W. Haney, W. Curtis Banks, and Philip G. Zimbardo (1973)

**NAME OF REPLICATION/EXTENSION:** Rethinking the Psychology of Tyranny: The BBC Prison Study

**REPLICATION SCIENTIST/RESEARCH:** Stephen Reicher and Alexander Haslam (2006)

SOCIAL

Have you ever played a role? If you've never appeared in a school play or local theater production you may think that you haven't ever played any roles. But we play roles all the time. Have you ever been the president of a club? A referee for a local sports team? A babysitter? Teacher? These are all roles. What makes them roles is that there are expected behaviors that go along with them. When you're the "teacher" you feel that it's your job to keep order in the class and to make sure students pay attention to you. When you're a babysitter you know that the child's parents expect a certain level of "seriousness" from you. Club presidents are supposed to be serious and outgoing. We may not really have these characteristics, but when we play a role we have to act the way we know we're supposed to act.

But does it go deeper than "just an act"? When you're placed in a role and it's not going well—the kids in the classroom aren't paying attention to you, the baby is acting out, and the club members don't seem to respect you—does that "hurt" at a deeper level? Can these roles, which we know we're only playing temporarily, actually affect us deeply? Zimbardo's study is difficult to replicate, but Reicher and Haslam were able to do something similar to Zimbardo's study and they found some interesting results in their "BBC Prison Study." But for our purposes we'll focus on the power that roles can have over our emotions.

## THE ORIGINAL EXPERIMENT

Zimbardo and his colleagues at Stanford University wanted to answer those questions. They decided to use the roles of "prisoner" and "guard" in a prison setting. They created a fake prison in the basement of one of the buildings on the Stanford campus. They selected twenty-four male students and randomly assigned them to be either a "prisoner" or a "guard." The prisoners were given numbers and clothes similar to what a prisoner would wear and the "guards" were given uniforms and dark sunglasses to wear. At first, the guards played their roles the way they thought they were supposed to, by putting the "prisoners" in their cells. It was a friendly atmosphere at first, but as the study went on for a few days, things changed. Very quickly the guards became demanding and mean to the prisoners and the prisoners started to do things real prisoners do—shout at the guards, swear at them, and not do what they were told. In addition to these actions, it became clear that the students were "taking on" the role in a very deep emotional way. They were getting very upset and very angry and many had to be removed from the study early because of the strength of their emotional response. Clearly, when we take on a role, it can become more than just "doing what you're supposed to do." Playing the role can affect us.

## LET'S TRY IT!

There is a way to explore the effect of roles on our emotions without seriously endangering or upsetting anyone as in the Stanford study. Let's use a situation you're probably quite familiar with from school: having to work with other students on a group project. Students usually don't like to work in groups because typically one or two students do most of the work while the others slack off. Psychologists call this "social loafing." One way to combat this problem is by giving everyone in the group a role. Typical roles are "leader," "timekeeper," "notetaker," and "devil's advocate." These roles help group members keep focused and more productive.

Here is what you'll need:

- 4 friends
- Stopwatch

**WHAT TO DO:**
- **STEP 1:** Gather together some of your friends and tell them that you want them to work as a group for 5 minutes and to come up with as many possible uses as they can think of for a brick. This idea ("How many uses can you come up with for a brick") is very commonly used in research. You can use another topic—the idea is simply that you need to get your group members working on a task of some kind.
- **STEP 2:** Assign each person, in private, one of the following roles. You can write down each of these on a separate piece of paper to give to the person you've selected. Make sure that nobody knows what anyone else's role is.

  1. You're the group Leader and you're really enthusiastic about your ideas.

2. You're the group Timekeeper and you think your job is really, really important. So remind people of this frequently (along with telling them the amount of time left for the activity).

3. You're the group's "Devil's Advocate"—you make sure that any idea that is brought up is criticized. Always point out why the idea is no good.

4. You're the group's Note-taker—you write down the ideas but make sure it's clear that if it wasn't your idea you think the idea stinks.

- **STEP 3:** After you have spoken privately to everyone about their roles, sit everyone around a table and tell the timekeeper to say "Go" when he or she is ready.

## THE RESULTS

When the 5 minutes are up you can take a look at the ideas they wrote down, but you're really more interested in how they felt about each other. Ask each person to reveal what role was assigned to them and ask them to describe how they felt about the other people in the group. I'm betting that you'll find a lot of frustration comes out. The Leader probably found the Devil's Advocate to be annoying. The Devil's Advocate probably found the Note-taker annoying, and the Timekeeper probably annoyed everybody. The roles that the group members were assigned were only temporary and artificial—but nonetheless, people really get into their roles in ways that have emotional consequences.

## WHY IT MATTERS

All of us typically think that other people do what they do because of their personality. What we discover here is that sometimes we do what we do because that's what we think we're supposed to do to fulfill the role we've been placed in. And we take that job seriously. The Stanford prison study has been applied to real situations such as the American guards at Abu Ghraib who tortured Iraqi soldiers. These were ordinary people when they joined the armed forces, yet their behavior is difficult to accept. How much of their behavior are they responsible for and how much of it arises from the role they were placed in as guards?

# WHEN TRYING REALLY HARD MAKES NO DIFFERENCE

## *I GIVE UP!*

**PSYCH CONCEPT:** Cognitive Psychology

**NAME OF EXPERIMENT:** Failure to Escape Traumatic Shock

**ORIGINAL SCIENTIST/RESEARCH:** Martin Seligman and Steven Maier (1967)

**NAME OF REPLICATION/EXTENSION:** Learned Helplessness at Fifty: Insights From Neuroscience

**REPLICATION SCIENTIST/RESEARCH:** Steven Maier and Martin Seligman (2016)

COGNITION

Why do we all feel "depressed" from time to time? Why do other people feel this way very often? And when you feel this way, is there anything you can do to feel better? As with all human behavior and emotions, there are many causes. Cognitive-behavioral psychologists try to answer this question by focusing on your past experiences and on your current thoughts. If, in the past, you tried to get out of a difficult situation and you were unsuccessful in doing so, might you approach new difficult situations today with a sense of helplessness? Have you "learned to be helpless"? If so, perhaps the way to help you feel better is to help you have successful experiences today and to help you become more aware of the negative things you're saying to yourself. Maybe there's a way to make you feel less helpless—this is what Maier and Seligman have been looking at for over fifty years.

## THE ORIGINAL EXPERIMENT

Seligman and his colleagues wanted to find out what would happen if dogs were placed into difficult situations that were inescapable. They created cages that had wire floors, and these floors could be electrified with mild, but certainly annoying shocks. Some of these cages were built such that the dog could escape the shock by jumping over to a section of the cage that did not have an electric floor. Other dogs could not escape the shock no matter what they did.

What would the dogs in the "no escape" situation do if they were placed into a cage in which they now could escape by jumping into the non-electrified section? Wouldn't they jump over to that section? The answer was no. They had learned that they could not do anything to change their fate in the previous situation and even when they were now in a new situation they did nothing to even try to escape the shock. They had learned to be helpless.

## LET'S TRY IT!

There is a way to test this idea without having to shock any dogs. The key idea behind Seligman and Maier's work is that the dogs were put into an uncomfortable situation that they could not escape no matter how hard they tried. We can do this with our friends—as long as we do so in a respectful way.

The first thing we have to do is find a challenging activity for our subjects to work on. The activity often used, because most people are familiar with it, is the solving of anagrams. An anagram is simply a word whose letters can be rearranged to form another word or words. The letters in the word "canoe," for example, can be rearranged to form the word "ocean." If you search the web on the terms "list of easy and hard anagrams" you'll find plenty of websites that will give you anagrams you can use in this study.

For this experiment you're going to need:

- 8–10 friends
- 2 relatively easy anagrams, such as tubs (bust), vein (vine), and agree (eager)
- 2 hard anagrams, such as signature (a true sign) and dynamite (may it end)
- 1 moderately difficult anagram, such as panels (naples)

**WHAT TO DO:**
- **STEP 1:** Print out one piece of paper that lists your words—numbered 1–3—in this order: Easy, Easy, Moderate. List the words from 1–3, but leave 10 blank lines between each word. Then create a piece of paper that lists your words in this order: Hard, Hard, Moderate. Again leave 10 blank lines between each word.
- **STEP 2:** Now, get your group of friends together in a room and tell them that you're going to ask them to solve some anagrams. You'll probably need to explain and give an example. Have them sit far enough apart from each other that they will not be able to see what's written on someone else's paper.
- **STEP 3:** Give half of your friends a copy of the piece of paper that that has the words listed in the Easy, Easy, Moderate order. The other half should get the paper that lists them in the Hard, Hard, Moderate order. Put the papers face down so they cannot see what's on the other side.
- **STEP 4:** Tell them that you're going to say "Begin" in a minute and that at that time they should turn their paper over and try to figure out the first anagram. When they think they've figured it out they should not look at the next word—they should simply turn their paper over and raise their hand. Tell them that when most people have figured it out you'll say "Stop," and those who haven't finished should turn their papers over. No one should shout out what the anagram was. You'll tell them the solutions to the anagrams when

the activity is over. Otherwise the room should be silent during this activity.

- **STEP 5:** Ask if there are any questions and then say "Begin." When half of them have their papers turned over and their hands raised (which will most likely be the Easy group) say, "Stop. Everyone turn their papers face down."
- **STEP 6:** Then say, "When I say 'Begin,' turn your papers over and try to solve anagram number 2. Begin." You'll probably see some frustrated faces from your Hard group. Again, after the hands are up and the papers turned over (mostly from the same people), say "Stop. Everyone turn their papers face down." You'll see more signs of disbelief and frustration from your Hard group members.
- **STEP 7:** Next say, "When I say 'Begin,' turn your papers over and try to solve anagram number 3. Begin." At this point all your subjects are trying to solve the same anagram (panels), but half of them have a history of failure.

## THE RESULTS

You'll find that those who had the two easy anagrams will probably solve the third one without much trouble. Those given the hard anagrams will probably not have solved them or the final anagram—even though everyone had the same task. Why? Because they have "learned helplessness." When we experience a lot of failure we don't expect to succeed and we give up—even when there might have been a good chance that we would have succeeded.

## WHY IT MATTERS

We have probably all felt a sense of learned helplessness in our lives. Students get frustrated when their teachers promise that they will be given a chance to participate in which book they will read, but then are assigned a book. After an experience like that the students are much less likely to even try to participate in class. Voters who hope to see improvements in their lives will go to the voting booths with enthusiasm in their early years, but sadly, after seeing many years go by with no change in their lives, many people stop voting altogether. This happens even during an election when there is a candidate who might have made a difference.

# HOW ANONYMITY CAN MAKE US MEAN

## *"THAT IS THE STUPIDEST THING YOU EVER SAID!"*

**PSYCH CONCEPT:** Deindividuation

**NAME OF EXPERIMENT:** The Human Choice: Individuation, Reason, and Order versus Deindividuation, Impulse, and Chaos

**ORIGINAL SCIENTIST/RESEARCH:** Philip Zimbardo (1969)

SOCIAL

If you have spent any time at all on the Internet (and who hasn't?) you've seen comments from people who are often referred to as "trolls." These are people who like to leave mean comments on YouTube videos, Instagram images, tweets, etc. Why do they do this? One explanation is that these are adolescents (typically male) who are trying to gain a sense of power from putting other people down. Another explanation involves the anonymity that the Internet gives us. Many people create usernames that are some combination of their first and last names, but you could of course just call yourself "zyx19375" or some other odd combination of letters and numbers, and in doing so you'd be completely anonymous. Psychologists have found that when we know we are anonymous we do things we wouldn't ordinarily do.

If you've ever been to a sports game you may find yourself acting in ways you don't normally act. This is partly caused by simply getting caught up in the excitement of the game, but it's also because you can yell things you wouldn't want your mother to hear and few people will know that it came from you. When we're anonymous we can do things we may not be proud of.

## THE ORIGINAL EXPERIMENT

Philip Zimbardo, who conducted the famous prison study covered in this book, also took a look at the idea of *deindividuation*. This is the observation that people will act in unexpected—and sometimes antisocial—ways when they feel a sense of anonymity. In daily life we all inhibit ourselves in some ways; that is, we often don't say what's really on our minds. When your boss criticizes you for something, you probably don't say the first things that comes to mind.

What are you capable of doing if nobody knows it's you? That's what Zimbardo wanted to find out.

Zimbardo did something quite straightforward: he brought subjects into a lab and gave them an opportunity to deliver a small shock to another person. That person was identified as being either a "nice" person or an "obnoxious" person. Some of the subjects were first given name tags when they arrived for the study (to increase their sense of identity) while others agreed to put on a lab coat and a hood so their true identity could not be known (they were "deindividuated" in this way). While the people with name tags delivered lower-intensity shocks to the nice person than to the obnoxious person, the subjects wearing the coat and hood delivered longer and higher-intensity shocks to both the nice and the obnoxious people.

So we will do some surprising things when we feel anonymous.

## LET'S TRY IT!

Okay, so you won't be shocking anyone. Instead let's apply this idea to an activity you see all the time: responses to social media posts.

While most social media posts on Facebook and Twitter are dull and harmless, sometimes people do say things that are surprisingly, well, ignorant. And humorous.

For example:

- "What the heck is Obama's last name anyway?"
- "I want my first daughter to be a girl."
- "Why do women never have to take a DNA test to see if the baby is theirs?"

No doubt you've seen some of these posts. You laugh and you may want to respond with an insult—but you usually don't. And you don't because you know that people would see your name and might think that you're being mean.

So here's what we'll need for our experiment:

- 2 groups of participants (about 5–10 people in each group)
- Paper for each participant with 3 outrageous posts and room to comment on each one
- Writing implements for participants
- Camera

You can use the posts listed previously or have some fun and do a web search on the words "dumbest things people say online." You'll get plenty of posts to choose from.

### WHAT TO DO:

Here's basically what you'll do: you'll have two groups and each person will have a piece of paper with 3 posts printed on it with a little space in between each one. You'll ask your friends to read each post as if they had seen it online or on their phone and then you'll ask them to write down how they would respond to the post. The catch? You'll make it obvious to one group of friends that their identity would be known by anyone who reads the comment and you'll hide the identity of your other friends. Let's dive in.

## GROUP A: HIGH-IDENTITY GROUP

- **STEP 1:** Each subject should come into your office (or sit at your table) individually. Tell him you're studying people's behavior in social media. Ask him to create a username just for this study that is a combination of his first and last names. Probably he'll create something like "John_Smith."

- **STEP 2:** Write down his username on a piece of paper and have him hold up the paper below his face while you take his photo. If he asks why you're doing this, just say that you want to make sure you can identify everyone's comments.

- **STEP 3:** Turn over the paper with the posts and tell your subject that you're going to ask him to read an actual post that someone put online, and then ask him to write down what he would say in response. Do this for all three posts.

- **STEP 4:** After your subject has written down his responses to the posts, he is done. Thank him, let him know you'll tell him your results when the study is over, and go on to your next person.

## GROUP B: DEINDIVIDUATED GROUP

- **STEP 1:** You're going to make these people feel anonymous. Ask them to create a username but make sure it would be impossible for anyone to figure out who the subject was. Suggest a combination of random numbers and letters. Don't take their pictures. This should allow these friends to feel pretty anonymous.

- **STEP 2:** Turn over the paper with the posts and tell your subject that you're going to ask her to read an actual post that someone put online, and then ask her to write down what she would say in response. Do this for all three posts.

- **STEP 3:** After your subject has written down her responses to the posts, she is done.

## THE RESULTS

When you've put about twenty people through your study (ten in each condition), you're done. Now the interesting part: reading the comments they've written. Try to do this without knowing which group the subject was in. See if you can guess which group they were in based on the amount of "meanness" in their comments. I think you'll find that those who thought they were anonymous wrote comments that were meaner than those who thought their identity could be figured out.

## WHY IT MATTERS

While I hope you had a little fun with this experiment, you should realize that there are serious side effects of online anonymity. Mean comments occur so often that the term "cyberbullying" has appeared to describe just how hurtful anonymous commenters can be. This is why many sites will not allow you to comment unless you create an account with information about yourself that could be used to personally identify you if someone notices that your comments were inappropriate. All social media companies are now involved in trying to find ways to lessen the hurt that people could cause when they know they're anonymous.

# WHY YOU CHOOSE YOUR ROMANTIC PARTNER IS LESS ROMANTIC THAN YOU THINK

## *YOU DIRTY DOG!*

**PSYCH CONCEPT:** Mating Strategies

**NAME OF EXPERIMENT:** Dog Ownership Increases Attractiveness and Attenuates Perceptions of Short-Term Mating Strategy in Cad-Like Men

**ORIGINAL SCIENTIST/RESEARCH:** Sigal Tifferet, Daniel J. Kruger, Orly Bar-Lev, and Shani Zeller (2013)

SOCIAL

Why are you romantically interested in someone? We like to think that our interests in another person have to do with their looks (at least at first) or their personality. Some psychologists, however, take a position that may seem rather blunt, but their research into the mysteries of love and attraction finds that these magical feelings often boil down to a pretty hard fact: women carry the babies. As we also know, human babies are a lot of work. When a woman gets pregnant she has to carry the little squiggler for around nine months. Then she has to feed and nurture it. It'll still be a year or so before it can even walk and maybe eighteen years before it can "leave the nest." In short, having sex involves the risk of getting pregnant, and having a child requires a lot of investment. So a woman has to be a lot more careful than a man about who she chooses for a partner. She's looking for someone who'll stick around for the long term and help care for the child.

Of course it's not always this straightforward. Women are not always looking to have children with a potential partner. So their "mating strategy" can be hard to predict. But that doesn't stop psychologists from trying to predict it!

How do dogs fit into all this? Let's see.

## THE ORIGINAL EXPERIMENT

Single men are often told that one way to attract the ladies is to get a dog and take it for walks in the park. What does owning a dog signal to other people? As we know, dogs require more care than cats. So if a single man owns a dog, does this mean that he's capable of other, longer-term relationships? Tifferet and her colleagues decided to find out what effect dog ownership had on women's perceptions of a man's attractiveness. But they also wanted to take into account the fact that women are sometimes looking for a man who'll make good "dad mate-rial" and sometimes they looking for a short-term relationship.

So here's what they did in their clever study: they showed women pictures of a man either walking or not walking a dog. They also described this man in a short paragraph in such a way that he was pre-sented as either good "dad" material or a "cad." A "cad," if you're not familiar with the term, is used to describe a man who is usually single, free spirited, and looking for casual relationships. Definitely not dad material.

So what did they find? Well, as expected, a man who was described as having "dad" qualities was seen as attractive for a long-term rela-tionship. It didn't matter if he was walking a dog. The "cad" in general was not perceived to be attractive for a long-term relationship, but it turns out that the advice about walking a dog in the park is right: his attractiveness went up if he was walking a dog. The dog was indeed a signal that even someone who appears to be a "cad" could be capable of sticking around for the long haul.

**LET'S TRY IT!**

This study isn't hard to test, but unlike most other studies in this book, this one is going to have four groups instead of two:

1. People who read about a dad and see a picture of him in which he doesn't have a dog
2. People who read about a dad and see a picture of him with his dog
3. People who read about a cad and see a picture of him in which he doesn't have a dog
4. People who read about a cad and see a picture of him with his dog

Another way to look at this study is this:

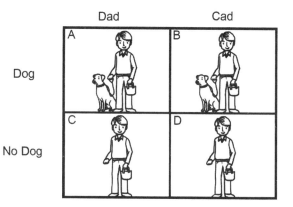

How do you carry out a study like this? Here's what you'll need:

- Attractive fellow
- Dog

- Location that looks like it could be a park
- Camera or smartphone to take a picture
- Descriptions of a dad and a cad
- 4 groups of 10 participants each

**WHAT TO DO:**

- **STEP 1:** Try to create the four conditions that you see in the image. Have your attractive fellow standing in a park, smiling and holding a dog leash with the dog sitting next to him. Then have him "freeze" while you remove the dog and the leash. Take his picture again.
- **STEP 2:** Now you'll need to prepare four pieces of paper for each of the four conditions:

1. Paper 1—a photo of your friend with a dog and this "dad" description: Roy is an accountant in his twenties. In his free time he likes to hike in nature. In addition, Roy likes to care for his dog, read, and play guitar.
2. Paper 2—a photo of your friend without a dog and this "dad" description: Roy is an accountant in his twenties. In his free time he likes to hike in nature, read, and play guitar.
3. Paper 3—a photo of your friend with the dog and this "cad" description: Roy is an accountant in his twenties. In his free time he enjoys playing sports and meeting friends at bars and cafes. In addition, Roy likes to care for his dog and go to concerts.
4. Paper 4—a photo of your friend without the dog and this "cad" description: Roy is an accountant in his twenties. In his free time he enjoys playing sports and meeting friends at bars and cafes. In addition, Roy likes going to concerts.

- **STEP 3:** Underneath each photo and description of your attractive man place these two 10-point scales:

> Based only on this information alone,
> how interested might you be in marrying this man?
> Not At All   **1   2   3   4   5   6   7   8   9   10**   Very Much

> Based only on this information alone,
> how interested might you be in having a "fling" with this man?
> Not At All   **1   2   3   4   5   6   7   8   9   10**   Very Much

- **STEP 4:** Show one picture to each of your groups and have them rate your man.

## THE RESULTS

Average up the scores for your subjects' responses in each of the four conditions. You'll probably find that the "dad" is perceived as good marriage material (gets a score of 7 or above) with or without a dog. The "dad's" scores are probably low on the "fling" question with or without a dog.

The "cad," on the other hand, will probably get a higher score than the dad on the "fling" question and a higher score on the "marry" question when your subjects see him with a dog. The "cad" will probably get a low score on the "marry" question when he isn't shown with a dog.

## WHY IT MATTERS

One of the biggest decisions you'll make in your life is, of course, who you decide to partner up with. We like to think that such decisions are based on immeasurable things like "love," and certainly that plays a part. But you have to admit that when it comes to figuring out if a partner is right for a long-term relationship, mixed in with all those great feelings is your perception of how well your potential partner is going to fulfill his or her role when it comes to the everyday facts of married life: washing dishes, caring for children, and keeping a job. Dog ownership appears to be one signal to women that a man is capable of a serious relationship.

# THE POWER OF CONFORMITY

## HOW MUCH WOULD YOU PAY FOR THAT CORNFLAKE?

**PSYCH CONCEPT:** Conformity

**NAME OF EXPERIMENT:** Group Forces in the Modification and Distortion of Judgments

**ORIGINAL SCIENTIST/RESEARCH:** Solomon Asch (1952)

SOCIAL

Let's face it—most of us want to know what everybody else thinks or what everybody else does before we do anything public. Before you buy a TV or a computer or even a blender you probably check to see how other people have rated the device on an online shopping site. Manufacturers know this, and that's why they encourage you to rate their products using 5-star scales and to share your happy experience with others.

But how far does this desire to "do what other people do" extend? Would you doubt your own eyes—your own sense of reality—if other people saw things differently than you do? That's what Solomon Asch wanted to find out, and we're going to try it out ourselves.

## THE ORIGINAL EXPERIMENT

Asch set up a pretty simple experiment. He brought small groups of college students (5–7) into a room. He told them that he was doing a "vision test" and then showed everyone a large card that had vertical black lines on it. The lines were labeled A–C. There was a separate card with a single vertical black line on it that was not labeled. Asch simply asked each group member in turn to say out loud which line on the card with the lettered lines was the same length as the line on the other card.

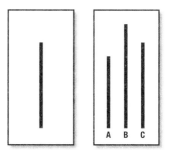

*Sample card from the Asch conformity experiments*

Since this was not really a "vision test" but one in psychology there was something else going on here. Among a group of, say, five students, there was actually only one true subject. The other four had met before the study with Asch and he told them which answers to give. He told them to say out loud the wrong answers regarding which line was equal in length to another line. The true subject didn't know that his teammates were giving the wrong answers. Asch found that when it came to the subject's turn (which was usually the last of the five), on average a little over a third of the time the true subject shook his head, looked at the others as if they were crazy, but then went along with them and gave the same wrong answer they did. This didn't happen in every instance, but often enough to show that some participants gave a clearly wrong answer just because everyone else was giving it.

What might you (or your friends) do just because everybody else is doing it? Let's find out in this fun little experiment.

## LET'S TRY IT!

Have you ever used one of those online auction sites like eBay or watched a television shopping channel? If you have, then perhaps you have been surprised at how much money people pay for products that really don't appear to be worth it. The reason they do this is in part because of what Asch discovered. When other people buy something—especially when it's a lot of other people doing so—we get caught up in the moment (which some people call "emotional contagion") and we feel compelled to do what others are doing.

But what if, as in Asch's study, it's pretty clear that everybody is saying something that appears really odd to you? Will you doubt your own perceptions and go along with the crowd? For example, some people have paid money on these auction sites for a "bottle of air." Would you?

So here's what we'll do: go online and find pictures of things that most everyone has found worthless but which other people have bought in an online auction. Here are a few things I found by searching for "weird things people have sold online":

1. A piece of toast
2. A stone shaped like a foot
3. Elephant dung
4. A cornflake shaped like the state of Illinois
5. An imaginary friend (the photo of this was simply an empty corner of a room)
6. A rock

Feel free to use these objects or find your own.
Here's what you'll need:

- Pictures of 5 objects
- 5 participants

## WHAT TO DO:

- **STEP 1:** Get your five participants together, but, like Asch, talk with four of them beforehand to set up what you want them to do.
- **STEP 2:** You're going to ask your participants to look at each picture individually and say out loud how much they would bid for that object if they saw it online. All the objects are worthless, but have

your four "fake" subjects agree to a price before the whole group gets together. You don't want a price that's outrageously high, like $2,000 for any object, but certainly a price that the average person would consider high (perhaps $5 for a piece of toast).

- **STEP 3:** Show them the pictures and let the first four participants give roughly the same high bid for each object. Your true subject will probably object to the prices and say something like, "Are you guys crazy?" So make sure your four cohorts are ready with something a little silly to say, like "I think that toast has a face in it—that's rare," or "I don't know, I think a cornflake shaped like a state is really cool."

## THE RESULTS

Make sure when you're done showing the five photos that you let the true subject in on the gag. He probably will suspect that something weird was going on. Researchers have found when they replicate Asch's study that conformity rates are lower among people today. We're just not as naturally conforming as Asch's students were in the 1950s. Still, I'll bet that the participants who didn't know what was going on will tell you that during the "bidding" process they were beginning to have major doubts about themselves.

## WHY IT MATTERS

Despite how much we say about how we "march to the beat of our own drummer" we often look to other people to see what we're "supposed" to do and think. Nobody wants to look foolish. On the other hand, what Asch and others also found is that it only takes one person in a crowd to not go along with what everyone else is doing to greatly decrease conformity. That one person can confirm what all the others are thinking but are not saying. With just one "block" pulled out, the whole house falls down. If you know you're right about something, don't assume that other people's silence means they are all in agreement. One way to find out what's really going on is to say something like, "What a minute . . . let me just play devil's advocate here. I think we might be wrong about this." If other people think so too, you've given them a way to stop conforming and express their opinion.

# WHAT MAKES US TRULY HAPPY?

## *THROW AWAY YOUR TVS FOLKS*

**PSYCH CONCEPT:** Happiness/Emotions
**NAME OF EXPERIMENT:** To Do or to Have? That Is the Question
**ORIGINAL SCIENTIST/RESEARCH:** Leaf Van Boven and Thomas Gilovich (2003)

COGNITION

Everybody wants the answer to this question: what can I do to be happier? Psychologists actually do have a few answers to that question. The first one involves how you spend your money. Most people think that if they win the lottery they will be happy. As it turns out, this isn't quite so. You might be happy to know that rich people aren't necessarily happier than non-rich people. We all "habituate" to what we have. If you've ever bought a new car or a new TV then you've experienced habituation; after a few months the excitement wears off. So believe it or not, if you owned a big house and drove a fast car it would indeed be very cool—for a little while. But nobody stays excited for the rest of his life. We all come "back down to earth."

So if habituation happens to everyone, what can you do to make positive experiences last longer? As it turns out, the best way to do this is to put your money into experiences instead of into things. That is, spend your money on a trip, or on a big birthday party for a friend. These experiences will leave long-lasting positive memories that will at least make you feel "warm" for years.

Let's find out how researchers discovered this.

## THE ORIGINAL EXPERIMENT

This experiment really wasn't very complicated. What Van Boven and Gilovich did was to ask college students to reflect on either a recent "experiential purchase," which they defined as "spending money with the primary intention of acquiring a life experience" such as a trip, or a "material purchase" such as a TV or car or other product.

After identifying the purchase and reflecting on it a bit, people were asked questions to identify how much happiness the purchase gave them. Sure enough, those people who reflected on the experiential purchase scored more highly on the questions about their happiness.

Let's go ahead and replicate this study.

## LET'S TRY IT!

Here's what you'll need:

- 2 groups of people
- Paper with questions

### WHAT TO DO:

#### GROUP A: EXPERIENTIAL PURCHASE

- **STEP 1:** Ask these folks to reflect on a recent experiential purchase they made. The purchase should have cost $100 or more. This is so you know that people really made an investment in the purchase. Spending a couple of bucks wouldn't count as an "experience." Ideally, an experiential purchase is also one in which the person spent time with others as well. Ask them to tell you a little about the experience.
- **STEP 2:** Print out the questions listed in this step on a piece of paper. When all of your subjects are done reflecting on their respective experiences, ask them to circle a number on each scale.

When you think about this purchase, how happy does it make you?

| 1 | 2 | 3 | 4 | 5 | 6 | 7 | 8 | 9 |
|---|---|---|---|---|---|---|---|---|
| Not happy | | | Moderately happy | | | | Extremely happy | |

How much does this purchase contribute to your happiness in life?

| 1 | 2 | 3 | 4 | 5 | 6 | 7 | 8 | 9 |
|---|---|---|---|---|---|---|---|---|
| Not at all | | | Moderately | | | | Very much | |

To what extent would you say this purchase is money well spent?

| 1 | 2 | 3 | 4 | 5 | 6 | 7 | 8 | 9 |
|---|---|---|---|---|---|---|---|---|
| Not well spent | | | Moderately well spent | | | | Very well spent | |

To what extent do you think the money spent on this purchase would have been better spent on something else—some other type of purchase that would have made you happier?

| 1 | 2 | 3 | 4 | 5 | 6 | 7 | 8 | 9 |
|---|---|---|---|---|---|---|---|---|
| Not at all | | | Moderately | | | | Very much | |

- **STEP 3:** When they're done, put an E on the back of each paper so you know that you asked this person to reflect on an experiential purchase. Feel free to tell the members of this group what your study is about—just ask them not to talk to the others about the study until you're done.

## GROUP B: MATERIAL PURCHASE

- **STEP 1:** Ask these folks to reflect on a recent material purchase they made. The purchase should have cost $100 or more.
- **STEP 2:** After they're done telling you about the purchase, give them the same questions as you did for group A and ask them to circle a number on each scale.
- **STEP 3:** When they're done, put an M on the back of each paper so you know that you asked this person to reflect on a material

purchase. Again, feel free to tell the group members what you expect to find regarding happiness.

## THE RESULTS

Notice that question 4 is a little different from questions 1–3. If the theory is right that experiential purchases make you happier, then group A people should have chosen a high number on questions 1–3 and a lower number on question 4. That is, they will probably think that the money was well spent.

What you'll need to do when a question is worded this way is to reverse the scores before you calculate an average for all four questions. That is, if someone circled a 1, make that a 9. Likewise, change 2 to an 8, 3 to a 7, and 4 to a 6; leave 5 as a 5; change 6 to a 4, 7 to a 3, 8 to a 2, and 9 to a 1. Then you can add up the scores and take an average for each person. Finally, average up all the scores for each group. The experiential group should have a higher score, which means that the experience had a much more positive effect on them.

## WHY IT MATTERS

It's good to realize that we actually do know a bit about what makes us happy. There are so many material things that companies want us to believe will make us happy—but it's just not so. Spending time with friends and family (even though there can be some uncomfortable moments) will result in better, more satisfying lifetime memories than a new TV, which, as we know, you'll throw away after a couple years.

# PERSUASION TACTICS IN A RESTAURANT

## DON'T FORGET TO TIP YOUR SERVER!

**PSYCH CONCEPT:** Persuasion

**NAME OF EXPERIMENT:** Effect on Restaurant Tipping of Presenting Customers with an Interesting Task and of Reciprocity

**ORIGINAL SCIENTIST/RESEARCH:** Bruce Rind and David Strohmetz (2001)

SOCIAL

At one point or another you will probably have (or already had) a job that depends on customers' tips. For some jobs, such as a server in a restaurant or a bartender, most of your income comes from tips. So naturally people in these jobs are very interested in what they can do—in addition to providing great service of course—to get customers to give them a great tip. Time to bring in a little psychology.

Psychologists have found that, not surprisingly, customers tip more when they're in a good mood. So what can a server do to get customers in a good mood? Here are a few tactics that have been shown to work:

- Draw a "smiley face" on the bill
- Draw a "smiley face" and put your first name on the bill
- Draw a sun on the bill
- Touch the customer lightly on the shoulder
- Use "mimicry"; that is, read back the order to the customer (as opposed to just saying "Got it")
- Tell a joke

Here's another tactic: give customers a fun little task to do. The task should put them in a good mood and that should translate into a better tip. What kind of task? Let's take a look.

## THE ORIGINAL EXPERIMENT

Rind and Strohmetz carried out their experiment in a real restaurant. Servers working along with the researchers randomly selected some of their tables to receive a fun little task printed on a small piece of paper. The customers were asked to count the number of Fs in this sentence:

FINISHED FILES ARE THE RESULT
OF YEARS OF SCIENTIFIC STUDY
COMBINED WITH THE EXPERIENCE
OF MANY YEARS.

Many people only count 3 Fs. There are actually 6 Fs. Why do people get this wrong? The F in the word "of" sounds like a V and because of this we often skip over it. We're looking for the F sound—not the V sound. This may not be the most fun activity you've ever experienced but it's challenging and surprising, so it can put people in a good mood.

The task was given at the end of the meal to some tables of customers and not given to others. The researchers then calculated the percentage of the tip that each table gave to the server. Guess what? When the servers gave the customers the fun task, the tip left by those customers was about 20 percent higher than the tip given by the tables that did not receive the task. In dollars-and-sense terms, the servers would make about $297 a week without giving the task, but they would make $353 in tips if they used the task. Not bad.

Let's get a little adventurous and replicate this study. But this time we'll throw everything we've got at it. You'll see.

## LET'S TRY IT!

The only way to replicate a study like this is to set up a little restaurant yourself. You can do this inside your laboratory. And by laboratory I mean a room where you can set up a table or three and you can be the server at a cafe. We'll just serve dessert so you don't have to cook a whole meal. Here's what you'll need:

- Large room
- 1–3 tables
- Puzzle task printed on 3 (3 × 5) index cards
- Subjects/friends to be customers
- Fresh, good-quality desserts (no little yellow cakes, candy, or inexpensive pie)

### WHAT TO DO:

- **STEP 1:** Make your room up to look like a nice little cafe. Give it a fancy name. Three round tables with ironed white tablecloths would be nice.
- **STEP 2:** Invite your subjects/friends to come over to your cafe. Feel free to tell them you're doing a little study or that you're testing out some new recipes.
- **STEP 3:** Make sure to let them know that you will have to charge them for the food at your cafe—but only a couple of dollars (just to recoup your costs).
- **STEP 4:** When they arrive, you can seat one person per table, but your friends will have more fun if they play the game in groups of three. More than three is probably too many.
- **STEP 5:** You're playing the role of server. Give each table one dessert for everyone to share. Tell them to enjoy and that when they're done you'll come over with the bill.

- **STEP 6:** Before you come back out with the bill (for whatever it cost you to buy that dessert), randomly assign the person or table to either the "puzzle" group or the "no puzzle" group. You can just flip a coin if you wish—they get a puzzle if you get heads, and no puzzle if you get tails.
- **STEP 7:** Return to each table with your bill. If you're supposed to give the table a puzzle, do that. Stay there while the person or people at the table try to figure out the puzzle. Show them the answer if they don't figure it out.
- **STEP 8:** Let your subjects know that tips are allowable by writing something like "Gratuities are welcome" on the bill.
- **STEP 9:** If you're giving a bill to a "no puzzle" table, just say thank you and give them the bill.
- **STEP 10:** Make sure after you get their money that you keep track of how much tip money you received from each table, and whether each was a puzzle or no-puzzle table.

## THE RESULTS

Your final step is to add up your tip money from the puzzle and no-puzzle tables and see which gave you the most money. You'll probably find the same thing the original researchers did: that participating in a puzzle is fun, and people in a good mood leave a larger tip.

Feel free to go even further with this study (heck, you took the time to set up all those tables and buy the dessert). To get an even bigger tip at the puzzle tables, write your first name on the bill along with a smiley face and a sun.

## WHY IT MATTERS

If you ever do work as a server, this information will come in handy. Customers at all restaurants and stores are the objects of persuasion all the time. Grocery stores, for example, will put the food they want you to buy at eye level instead of at the very bottom or top. Researchers are working all the time to try to find subtle ways to get you to spend more of your hard-earned money. It's to your advantage to either use these tools yourself or simply be aware that they are being used on you. At least then you can decide to go along with it or not.

# SUPERNORMAL STIMULI

## *MY WHAT BIG EYES YOU HAVE!*

**PSYCH CONCEPT:** Supernormal Stimuli
**NAME OF EXPERIMENT:** The Study of Instinct
**ORIGINAL SCIENTIST/RESEARCH:** Nikolaas Tinbergen (1951)
**NAME OF REPLICATION/EXTENSION:** Supernormal Stimuli
**REPLICATION SCIENTIST/RESEARCH:** Deirdre Barrett (2010)

COGNITION

One of the most famous pictures you'll see in just about every psychology textbook is that of a man taking a walk outside, with a line of ducks behind him. The ducks are following him just as they would follow their mother. The man is Konrad Lorenz and what he's demonstrating is the idea of imprinting. He, along with Nikolaas Tinbergen, discovered that there is a critical period for many mammals, usually within the first day of life, when they will follow (or "imprint on") whatever large moving object happens to be in their presence. Normally of course that large object is their mother and it's a good thing this happens, because she will protect and guide them during their first few weeks of life.

Okay, so that's cute, you say, but what does that have to do with me? Well, actually a lot. This tendency to focus on abnormally large or unusual objects is used by food marketers to get you to buy products, and even by people who are trying to raise money. Let's find out how.

## THE ORIGINAL EXPERIMENT

Lorenz found that ducks could imprint on all kinds of abnormally large objects, like his boots. Large objects, or ones that are particularly bright or in other ways unusual, have a strong appeal to all kinds of animals. For example, Tinbergen found that mother birds have a tendency to pay more attention to the largest of their eggs. That makes sense for survival, since the baby bird that emerges from that egg is the one that will probably be the healthiest and the one most likely to live. So they wondered: would a mother bird pay more attention to a large egg made out of plaster? The answer is yes. Would they pay more attention to a real egg, but one that came from another species of bird? As odd as this sounds, the answer is again, yes.

More recently, psychologist Deirdre Barrett, in her book *Supernormal Stimuli*, has found that this "pull" we have toward objects that are unusual in some way—larger or more colorful than the normal object—explains why it's hard to resist being attracted to a baby or an animal with large eyes, or an overly large cookie, or a large muffin covered with icing, nuts, and chocolate.

Let's not let this knowledge "sit on the shelf." Let's use it to raise some money.

## LET'S TRY IT!

Let's try to raise money for the local SPCA. No doubt you've gone to a gas station and seen a jar with a picture of an animal on it and a message asking you to donate to the SPCA or some other good cause. Let's do a little experiment.

Here's what you'll need:

- 2 large, 12-ounce glass jars
- 2 small index cards
- Transparent tape
- 2 small pictures of a cat
- Image editing tool such as Photoshop Elements (and someone with a little familiarity with how to use it)
- Permission from 2 gas station managers to put your jars in their stores

**WHAT TO DO:**

- **STEP 1:** Using a felt-tip pen, write "Please donate to the SPCA" on each index card. Tape the index cards onto the inside of each jar.
- **STEP 2:** Get a digital photo of a cat and follow this process (https://vimeo.com/167731045) to make its eyes super normally large.
- **STEP 3:** Print out a picture of your cat with normally sized eyes and print out a picture of the cat with super normally large eyes.
- **STEP 4:** Tape one picture on the inside of one jar (next to the message about donating to the SPCA) and tape the other picture inside the other jar.
- **STEP 5:** Put one of the jars in one gas station and the other jar in the other gas station. Wait one week, then count how much money is in each jar.

## THE RESULTS

If the theory about supernormal stimuli is correct, you should have attracted more people with the picture of the cat with the large eyes, and hopefully that attention will translate into more money.

Of course, it's important that the two gas stations be as similar as possible in terms of how many customers they get during the week. That might be tough to find out, but welcome to the dilemma faced by social scientists when they do research in the "real world" instead of in a lab: it's hard to control all the possible factors that could affect your study.

## WHY IT MATTERS

The fact that you are drawn to supernormal stimuli is a fact that is used by marketers to get you to buy all kinds of products. In fact, Deirdre Barrett believes that this is one of the reasons for our current obesity epidemic: we find images of really attractive-looking food hard to resist. Whenever you see a really large cookie in a bakery, that's a supernormal stimulus—and it's hard not to be drawn to it.

Of course, you can use this tendency for good, as we've done here by using a cat with large eyes to raise money. You could use this idea to get more sales at your next bake sale. How about the next time you try to raise money by washing cars? Instead of holding up a sign that says "Car Wash," draw a picture of a car with really large eyes (headlights) and a sad look on its "face." You might be surprised at how many customers are drawn in by such an image.

# COGNITIVE DISSONANCE: WE SEE WHAT WE WANT TO SEE

## I WAS RIGHT ALL ALONG!

**PSYCH CONCEPT:** Cognitive Dissonance
**NAME OF EXPERIMENT:** Cognitive Consequences of Forced Compliance
**ORIGINAL SCIENTIST/RESEARCH:** Leon Festinger and James Carlsmith (1959)

COGNITION

Let's face it: we hate to be wrong. We also hate to be inconsistent. If at one time you're in favor of something and then at a different time you're against it, and someone points this out to you, you feel uncomfortable. It makes us feel embarrassed and it takes a certain strength of character to say that you had changed your mind or that you were wrong about what you said earlier.

This odd but strong tendency of ours can make us believe some pretty weird things. Festinger and Carlsmith carried out one of the more complex and counterintuitive studies in all of psychology. They wanted to find out what would happen if they could create a situation in which people contradicted themselves. How would they handle it?

## THE ORIGINAL EXPERIMENT

Festinger and Carlsmith first came up with a really, really boring activity. They gave subjects twelve spools (without the thread) and asked subjects to put the spools into a tray, then empty the tray, and then put the spools back into the tray. They did this for thirty minutes. Pretty boring, right? It gets worse. They then took away the spools and put a board in front of them that contained forty-eight pegs. They were asked to turn each peg a quarter-turn clockwise and then move on to the next peg and turn it a quarter-turn clockwise. When they reached the end of the pegs they should start over with the first peg and continue with this turning task. They were asked to do this for thirty minutes. Why? Because Festinger and Carlsmith wanted their subjects to have a really, really, boring experience. They succeeded.

Next came the tricky stuff: when the subjects were finished with the task they were told that the experimenter's assistant hadn't shown up that day and that the next subject was waiting in another room. They were asked to go to the next subject and tell him that the activity was really interesting. Some subjects were paid $1 to say this and others were paid $20 to say this.

When they were done talking to the next person who was waiting, the subjects went to another room, filled out a quick survey, and left. As part of the survey they were asked how interesting the activity was.

What do you think happened? Well, the subjects who were paid $20 said that the activity was really, really boring. Those who were paid only $1 thought that it really wasn't that bad.

What this means is that Festinger and Carlsmith succeeded in getting some people to contradict themselves. They had a really boring experience, but they told someone that it was really interesting. Those who were paid $20 had an excuse for saying that—they were paid well for doing what they did, so it didn't bother them too much that they did one thing and said another. Those who were paid $1 were left to feel a little uneasy. That uneasiness is what Festinger and Carlsmith called "cognitive dissonance." Those subjects resolved the uneasiness by convincing themselves that the task really wasn't that bad after all.

## LET'S TRY IT!

Now you might be saying to yourself, "Okay, that's a weird study. But what does it have to do with me?" Actually quite a lot, and you can prove this to yourself and to others.

Here's what you'll need:

- 1–2 friends
- Computer

**WHAT TO DO:**

- **STEP 1:** Ask friends about a purchase they made recently. Preferably this purchase was online and at a site where there are reviews from other people who also bought the product. It would be nice if the cost of the product was over $50, but that part isn't necessary.
- **STEP 2:** Sit down with your friends at a computer and go through the reviews—the positive ones and the negative ones. If a lot of the reviews are positive, then after reading a few positive ones go directly to read a few negative reviews. Pay particular attention to what your friends say about the negative reviewers' comments.

## THE RESULTS

What you'll find is this: your friends will find reasons not to have any confidence in the negative reviews. You may hear things like, "Oh, she doesn't know what she's talking about" or "That review doesn't make any sense." Your friends will probably read the negative reviews carefully just to find something they can criticize. But the reviewers who bought the product and like it, as your friends did, are seen as clearly very intelligent people.

Why do we do this? Because of what's called "post-decisional dissonance." We hate to think that we made a mistake. Once you've already bought the product, you want to think that you made a good choice and you want to think that any reviewer who says that it was a bad choice—no matter how good a point they make—is wrong.

Another way to test this out (but it'll cost you) is to buy three relatively inexpensive products that people buy every day (shampoo for example). Put three different brands of the product in front of your friends (one at a time). Tell them they can have any one they want. After they choose a brand, have your computer ready and go to a site like Amazon.com and have them read the comments. Once again, you'll find that they like the positive reviews (the people who agreed with their choice) and dislike the negative review.

## WHY IT MATTERS

As anyone will tell you, it's important to be honest with yourself. But often we just aren't. Our desire to feel good about ourselves and the decisions we make is very strong. Internal conflict is something we like to avoid. It's so strong that we'll often "bend" reality a little bit. We'll focus on what facts agree with what will make us look good and the facts that confirm that we made the right choice. Being honest with yourself takes some courage and the humility to admit that maybe, just maybe, you could have made a mistake.

# THE RORSCHACH INKBLOTS

## *TELL ME WHAT YOU SEE*

**PSYCH CONCEPT:** Personality Tests/Projective Tests
**NAME OF EXPERIMENT:** Psychodiagnostik
**ORIGINAL SCIENTIST/RESEARCH:** Hermann Rorschach (1948)

COGNITION

There are a few symbols that have become etched in our minds as representing the field of psychology; one of these is the infamous black-and-white "vase/faces" image. You'll see different things depending on whether you focus on the black part of the drawing or the white part. Another famous symbol is of course an inkblot. These inkblots, developed in 1921 by Hermann Rorschach, are rarely administered by psychologists anymore. This is especially so ever since the actual inkblots developed by Rorschach are now publicly available online.

Among psychologists, the key concern about the inkblots is what we call poor "inter-rater reliability." This means that when you show an inkblot to someone and they say something like "It looks like a bat," not every inkblot interpreter will agree as to exactly what that means about that person. Clearly, if someone sees sexual imagery in every inkblot he's shown, then that person probably does think about sex a lot. But this is rare. Most people see the exact same things in each blot. However, the idea does seem to make sense: we "project" some part of our inner selves onto these ambiguous images when we talk about what we see.

There's actually a very complex scoring system for the inkblots. This system goes way beyond whether or not you see a rat or a bat. Scorers look at whether or not you see the object moving, whether you use the part that is in color (they're not all black-and-white blots), how much of the total blot you focus on, how many parts of the image you focus on, and how common your answer is among all those who have looked at that blot. There's a great deal of training that goes into the scoring process. It's not an "off the cuff" kind of analysis that you might have seen in the movies.

So to properly score these inkblots the scorer must focus on the details and disregard what is not important. What we'll do in this study is to see how one unimportant detail—the person's name—can make people misinterpret someone's response to the test.

## THE ORIGINAL EXPERIMENT

Hermann Rorschach studied psychoanalysis, which was developed by Sigmund Freud. Freud believed that all of us have a tendency to "project" our feelings onto other people and things. That is, when we have thoughts or feelings we're uncomfortable with, we might imagine that someone else is thinking or feeling it. For example, suppose you feel very angry at one of your parents over something they did. You might also feel—though Freud would say that this feeling is unconscious—that it's wrong for you to ever be angry at your parents. So what you might do is have the thought that your *parent* is the one who's angry at *you*. You'd be taking the anger you feel and projecting it—like a movie projector—onto another person.

That's the idea behind the inkblots and other kinds of "projective" tests: you are given an ambiguous image or task (such as "Draw a person on this piece of paper") with the idea being that when you tell a psychiatrist or psychologist what you see in the ambiguous image—or what you draw on the paper—this will reveal something about your personality.

There has been a good deal of controversy over the years about whether these blots can help identify people with mental illnesses, but the consensus is that when a comprehensive scoring system is used (typically the one developed by psychologist John Exner), the test seems to be pretty reliable. However, the test is rarely used by itself. Psychologists always consider the results of the Rorschach test along with other tests and their interview with the person.

## LET'S TRY IT!

Of course, we can't do a study to see if we can identify mental illness in your friends. We'll leave that up to the professionals. However, we can take a look at something that has worried people over the years about these inkblots: are test interpreters objectively scoring the results of the test—or are they, like the patient, seeing what they want to see in a person's responses?

We'll show some inkblots to your subjects and we'll even provide some actual responses people have given to these blots. However, we're going to put different names on the blots. What many researchers have found is that some people's names are "desirable sounding"—such as Julie, Richard, and Gregory—while people respond less positively to names like Horace, Edmund, and Roderick.

Here is what you'll need:

- Printouts of inkblots I, IV, and V (more on this later)
- 2 groups of participants
- Rating scale for participants to write on
- Writing implements for participants

### WHAT TO DO:
- **STEP 1:** Go to Wikipedia in your web browser and find the actual inkblots used in the test (do a search on the words "Rorschach test"). Since the images are now in the public domain, all ten are available for download. Download the images for cards I, IV, and V (i.e, 1, 4, and 5).
- **STEP 2:** Print out each image on a separate piece of paper. Don't make the image too big on the paper. Make sure you have room at

the bottom to write a fictional name and a few responses to what the fictional person said about the inkblot (see step 3). Let's call your images 1, 2, and 3. Put the number of the image on the back of the paper.

- **STEP 3:** Underneath each inkblot image write the following:

    1. Underneath image 1, write: "I think that's a mask, or maybe an animal's face—or perhaps a jack o' lantern."
    2. Underneath image 2, write: "That looks like a monster to me. Or maybe it's a gorilla about to attack."
    3. Underneath image 3, write: "Those things at the top of the image are scissors I think. Or perhaps two people moving away from me. That could be crocodile heads in the bottom left and right."

The responses given here are a little unusual and might—and I do emphasize *might*—indicate that the person is troubled. Let's combine these answers with the positive and negative names and then ask our subjects how "stable" they think the person is.

### GROUP A: POSITIVE NAMES GROUP

- **STEP 1:** Underneath the quote for image 1, write "Julie."
- **STEP 2:** Underneath the quote for image 2, write "Richard."
- **STEP 3:** Underneath the quote for image 3, write "Gregory."
- **STEP 4:** At the bottom of the page ask your subjects to respond to this question by circling a number on the scale:

Based on this response to the inkblot,
how unstable do you think this person is?
Very Stable  **1  2  3  4  5  6  7  8  9  10**  Very Unstable

### GROUP B: LESS POSITIVE NAMES GROUP

- **STEP 1:** Underneath the quote for image 1, write "Horace."
- **STEP 2:** Underneath the quote for image 2, write "Edmund."

- **STEP 3:** Underneath the quote for image 3, write "Roderick."
- **STEP 4:** As with group A, at the bottom of every page ask your subjects to respond to this question by circling a number on the scale:

Based on this response to the inkblot,
how unstable do you think this person is?

Very Stable    **1   2   3   4   5   6   7   8   9   10**    Very Unstable

- **STEP 5:** Once your subjects have circled a number for all three inkblots, your study is complete.

## THE RESULTS

What you'll probably find is that your subjects circled lower "stability" numbers for the people with less positive-sounding names. Their judgment of the fictional person's mental health has been swayed by a fact that should be irrelevant: the person's name.

## WHY IT MATTERS

The Rorschach does seem to have some ability to identify individuals who suffer from some types of mental illnesses, but we must keep in mind three very important facts. The first is that the test is never used alone. What a person sees in the blots is always combined with other information about them. Second, the scoring system is far more complex than simply naming one thing in the image. On television you'll see someone say, "I see a butterfly," but the scoring systems for the Rorschach include all kinds of other information besides the main object the person sees. And finally, the person scoring the inkblots has to be carefully trained. They can't be influenced by things that easily influence everyday folks—like the sound or look of a person's name.

# HOW A PHONE CONVERSATION IS DIFFERENT FROM IN-PERSON

## SORRY! CAN'T TALK NOW

**PSYCH CONCEPT:** Inattentional Blindness

**NAME OF EXPERIMENT:** Passenger and Cell Phone Conversations in Simulated Driving

**ORIGINAL SCIENTIST/RESEARCH:** Frank A. Drews, Monisha Pasupathi, and David L. Strayer (2008)

**NAME OF REPLICATION/EXTENSION:** The Invisible Gorilla

**REPLICATION SCIENTIST/RESEARCH:** Christopher Chabris and Daniel Simons (2010)

SOCIAL

Over 14 million YouTube views: that's how popular the so-called "invisible gorilla" video has become since it was posted there in 2008. If you haven't seen it yet then you might want to go take a look. Look now, because I'm going to give away the ending in the next paragraph. You've been warned.

## THE ORIGINAL EXPERIMENT

Here's what the researchers did: for about thirty seconds you watch a video of a group of six college students in a hallway passing two basketballs among them. Three of the kids are in white shirts and three are in black. Before you watch the video you're told to focus on the students wearing the white T-shirts and to count the number of times they pass the ball. Pretty straightforward. What is hard to believe is that most people completely the miss the fact that in the middle of the video a person in a gorilla suit walks right through the kids passing the basketballs. How in the world could you possibly miss a man in a gorilla suit, you ask? But almost everybody does.

This is referred to as "inattention blindness." When we focus on something that is a little bit complex (such as counting the number of ball passes made by people wearing white T-shirts) we tend to let everything else we're not concerned with fade away so that we can focus on that task. We aren't expecting a gorilla to walk through the scene—nothing had even hinted that anything unusual might happen—so our attention is so focused that we can miss completely obvious things.

Here's another example. College students were asked to walk from one part of their campus to another while holding a cell phone conversation. Many of them completely missed a clown riding a unicycle. How could you miss a clown on a unicycle?

Researchers Drews, Pasupathi, and Simons found that when people were asked to hold a cell phone conversation while they were in a driving simulator they made more driving errors than people who held a similar conversation with a person sitting in the passenger seat. Why would this happen? A conversation is a conversation, right?

Well, as you know, the person on the cell phone has no idea what the driving conditions are that you are facing. They could be just sitting at home on their couch. Your passenger, however, can see exactly what's going on around you—whether there's a complex intersection up ahead, or that the car in front is taking a turn, or that a group of people are walking along the side of the road. Your passenger will pause during those times, or draw your attention to these events. This gives you the time and the "cognitive resources" you need to navigate the situation. Your friend on the cell phone, however, cannot see these things. That means that you have to pay attention to a lot more things going on around you. And you have to do a whole lot more thinking. And like trying to watch and count the number of ball passes being made by people in white T-shirts, you're going to miss something. You're more likely to have an accident.

## LET'S TRY IT!

Now, you could replicate the "gorilla" study pretty straightforwardly: shoot a thirty-second video of six of your friends while they pass a basketball among them in the hallway. Make sure three of them wear black shirts and three of them wear white. Oh yes, and rent a gorilla costume so your seventh friend can walk right through the basketball-tossing game. Show the video to your friends and ask them to count the number of passes made by the white- or black-shirted people. Probably not one of them will shout in the middle of the video, "Hey—what's that gorilla doing in there?"

But instead let's do something that will really drive an important point home about driving. Let's replicate the study by Drews and his colleagues. And for that we're going to put your cell phone to good use. Here's what you'll need:

- Smartphone (you could also use an Xbox or PlayStation game player)
- Driving simulator
- A friend to chat with
- A stopwatch

Both the iTunes and Android app stores have free (with ads) driving simulators. Download any one you like, though it would be great if the game kept track of any driving errors you make.

### WHAT TO DO:

### CONDITION A: IN-PERSON CONVERSATION
- **STEP 1:** Sit down at a table and ask your friend to sit next to you.
- **STEP 2:** Agree on a topic to discuss for 10 minutes.
- **STEP 3:** Start playing your driving simulator. Make sure that the road you're on is fairly complex—there's oncoming traffic, traffic lights, and so on. Start your stopwatch.

- **STEP 4:** Have your friend start talking to you while you both watch you driving the simulator.
- **STEP 5:** Drive for 10 minutes and the "study" is over.

### CONDITION B: PHONE CONVERSATION
- **STEP 1:** Agree with your friend on a topic to discuss for 10 minutes.
- **STEP 2:** Start playing your driving simulator. Make sure that the road you're on is fairly complex—there's oncoming traffic, traffic lights, and so on.
- **STEP 3:** Have your friend call you on the phone for the conversation. Since you'll be on your phone playing on the driving simulator, you'll probably have to have your friend call you on a landline. You can put the phone on speaker and put it down next to you as you drive the simulator. Start your stopwatch.
- **STEP 4:** Drive for 10 minutes and the "study" is over.

## THE RESULTS

If your driving simulator counts the number of mistakes you made during your ten-minute drive, or if it gives you a score, you'll probably find that your driving is worse when you talk to your friend on the phone.

## WHY IT MATTERS

Most of us think that "a conversation is a conversation." And that it doesn't matter if the person you're talking to is on the phone while you drive or sitting next to you in the car. Not so. Talking on a cell phone while you drive really is more dangerous than if the person was right next to you. Keep this in mind as you drive. Save the long conversations for when you get home so you can keep your attention on the road.

# REMEMBERING WHAT NEVER HAPPENED

## I KNOW WHAT I SAW! I THINK . . .

**PSYCH CONCEPT:** False Memories

**NAME OF EXPERIMENT:** Creating False Memories: Remembering Words Not Presented in Lists

**ORIGINAL SCIENTIST/RESEARCH:** Henry L. Roediger III and Kathleen B. McDermott (1995)

MEMORY

If there's a topic psychologists love to study it's memory. There are two reasons for this popularity: 1. It's not that hard to study memory—you just give participants a list of things to remember and then you wait a little bit and then ask them to write down what they remember. No fancy equipment needed. 2. What we find in our studies is so contradictory to what people think about their memories. People have such confidence in what they believe they've seen, and yet the evidence about the accuracy of their memories indicates that they really shouldn't be that confident. Let's look at an example of how easy it is to fool the memory.

## THE ORIGINAL EXPERIMENT

What if I got you in a room and told you that I would read out twelve words that I would later ask you to recall? I go ahead and read the twelve words out loud and then give you a paper and pencil and ask you to write down as many as you could remember. This is what Roediger and McDermott did, and they discovered a couple of things. First, to no one's surprise, people tend to mostly remember the first words they heard (this is called the primacy effect) and the last words they heard (the recency effect). But the researchers also did something a little tricky: the words were related in some way. Here's one list of words: table, sit, legs, seat, soft, desk, arm, sofa, wood, cushion, rest, stool. They're all pieces of furniture. When they read these words out loud they would find that words like chair, sit, and legs were remembered (the first three in the list) and the last three were remembered: cushion, rest, and stool.

But here's the tricky part. Look away from this page and answer this question: was the word "chair" in the list? A lot of people said yes, but the answer is no. Because the words are related, you assume that a word like "chair" was probably in the list. Here's another list of words: queen, England, crown, prince, George, dictator, palace, throne, chess, rule, subjects, monarch, royal, leader, reign. Now don't look back when you answer this question: was the word "king" in that list? Since you've gotten wise to what I'm doing here you probably said no and you're right—it wasn't. But many people said yes.

This study showed us that our memories are a mix of what we actually remember and what we think we saw. Here's a study you can readily replicate with your friends.

## LET'S TRY IT!

Here's what you'll need for this experiment:

- 2–4 participants
- List of 12 or 15 related words
- Piece of paper (for each subject you test) with 3 questions on it
- Writing implements for participants

Feel free to use the list of furniture- or monarchy-related words in the previous section, or the following spider-related list, which also was used by Roediger and McDermott.

- Web
- Insect
- Bug
- Fright
- Fly

- Arachnid
- Crawl
- Tarantula
- Poison
- Bite

- Creepy
- Animal
- Ugly
- Feelers
- Small

Here are the questions you'll need to have your participants answer:

1. List as many words as you can recall (leave some space after this question for them to write).
2. Was the word _____ on the list?
   Not on the list   **1 2 3 4**   Definitely on the list

3. Was the word _____ on the list?
   Not on the list   **1 2 3 4**   Definitely on the list

### WHAT TO DO:

- **STEP 1:** Read the list of words to your participants.
- **STEP 2:** Have your subjects write down as many words as they can recall (don't let them look at the others' answers if you're doing this in a group).
- **STEP 3:** Read questions 2 and 3 out loud, and fill in the blank as you read the questions. You'll want to fill in the blank in question 2 with a word that definitely was in the list; for question 3, read a word that definitely wasn't in the list. For the word that definitely was in the list, pick a word from the middle of the list so there is at least some uncertainty about it. For the spider-related list, you might use "crawl." For the house furniture list you could say a word that appeared in the middle of the list, which was "desk."

For question 3 pick a word that sounds like it should have been in the list but actually wasn't. For the spider-related list, say the word "spider"—it wasn't in the list. For the list of furniture, say the word "chair," which sounds like it ought to have been in the list but wasn't.

## THE RESULTS

You'll find that your subjects, like most people, remember more of the first and the last words that you read out loud. No surprise there. For question 2 there will be some hesitation, but most of them will circle either a 3 or a 4 (they think the word was in the list, and indeed it was). For question 3 you'll also find a lot of people who circle 3 and 4 even though those words weren't in the list. You could, of course, read more lists and even include another "fill in the blank" question in which you ask about whether some weakly related word was in the list. For example, in the furniture list, Roediger and McDermott asked whether the word "couch" was in the list. It wasn't, but your subjects will really rack their brains over that one.

## WHY IT MATTERS

This study shows how easy it is to create memories people are confident about, but which didn't really happen. Our memories are not photographic. When we "pull up" a memory we add to that memory what we think probably happened. You might say that the act of recalling words from a list you just heard is a lot different from recalling the details of a burglary or an accident. Roediger and McDermott agree. But they would point out that this study shows that we are able to create false memories in people who knew their memories were going to be tested. Yet they still made mistakes they were confident about. Why would our memories of a heightened situation that happens very, very quickly (like a car accident) be more accurate?

# HOW AND WHEN WE ARE BLIND TO CHANGE

## HOW COULD I HAVE MISSED SOMETHING LIKE THAT?

**PSYCH CONCEPT:** Change Blindness

**NAME OF EXPERIMENT:** Failure to Detect Changes to People During a Real-World Interaction

**ORIGINAL SCIENTIST/RESEARCH:** Daniel J. Simons and Daniel T. Levin (1998)

COGNITION

Once again, psychologists have found a situation in which what you think would be true simply isn't so. Here's the situation: you're walking down the street and someone asks you for directions. You say sure. Your attention is blocked only for a split second and when you look at the person again you don't notice any change. In fact, you're now talking to a completely different person. And you didn't even notice it happen. Don't believe this could happen? Let's find out why it happens and how we can reproduce this odd effect.

### THE ORIGINAL EXPERIMENT

Simons and Levin conducted a really simple study. Of course, they did it on a college campus (you'll notice that theme a lot in this book). The scenario: a person is standing in the middle of campus holding a map. He looks lost. He asks you for directions. You stop and agree to help. A second or so after you stop to help him a couple of guys say, "Coming through!" and they rudely walk right between the two of you holding a large door between them. Because of this, you can't see the other person for a second. When the guys with the door pass, you continue to help the lost man. What you didn't realize is the old "switcheroo" occurred: hidden from your view, the lost man you were helping was replaced with a completely different man who continued the conversation with you as if nothing happened. In many cases, subjects didn't notice a darn thing different. This is what has been called "change blindness."

It happens for a number of reasons:

- **The situation is ordinary.** You don't detect any danger in the surroundings. After all, you're just walking from one place to another, so you're not expecting anything weird. Your arousal level is low.
- **You have a "script" for situations like this.** You notice a "lost guy on campus." You'll look at his map, point in the direction he should go, and then you're on your way again. As a result of this script, you're not paying a whole lot of attention to what is really going on.
- **The person is a member of your "out-group."** Simons and Levin noticed that "blindness" was especially likely to occur if the person you're helping is easy to identify as not one of your "social identities."

We all have social identities. These are the groups we belong to. In this research, students were the subjects. They identified themselves as "students." This "blindness" was especially effective when the guy asking for help was clearly not a student. In one case Simons and Levin had the lost man dressed like a construction worker. As such, to a student he was clearly an "out-group member." We tend not to pay as much attention to out-group members as we do to members of our own group. When you don't pay much attention, weird things can happen that you don't notice. Sure enough, students were not at all likely to notice that the construction guy they were just talking to was just switched with a completely different construction guy.

Of course, Simons and Levin admit that there are limits to this "blindness." If the construction guy was replaced by another construction guy who was significantly taller or a completely different race from the guy you just saw (or a different gender), you would probably notice. Still, these studies show that you'd be amazed at how much we don't notice.

## LET'S TRY IT!

This study is pretty easy to replicate. If you search for the term "change blindness" on YouTube, you'll see how it's done. Here's a list of what you'll need:

- Location where a person might get lost. A college campus works well for this purpose, but a park would also work, or a not-too-crowded street.
- Large door
- 2 folding maps
- Lost Guy 1: a person to serve as your first "lost guy/girl"
- Lost Guy 2: another person who is somewhat similar to the first guy/girl (but not too much) to serve as your "replacement lost guy"
- 2 people to act as door carriers

### WHAT TO DO:
- **STEP 1:** Lost Guy 1 stands in the not-too-crowded spot and holds out the map. He should look lost.
- **STEP 2:** The door carriers are standing nearby, holding the door vertically. They could be talking or just look like they are waiting for someone. They are actually waiting for your real subject to come along to help. Lost Guy 2 stands behind the door with his map open. He is ready to walk along with the door as soon as your door carriers move.

- **STEP 3:** When someone comes near who looks like they might be helpful, Lost Guy 1 says something like, "Excuse me. I'm lost. Could you help me?"
- **STEP 4:** As soon as the subject (the "helper") comes to about 2 feet away from Lost Guy 1, the door carriers get on the move, with Lost Guy 2 walking behind the door.
- **STEP 5:** One door carrier shouts "Coming through!" as they turn the door sideways (Lost Guy 2 will have to duck a little to stay shielded by the door) and then walk right between the helper and Lost Guy 1.
- **STEP 6:** Lost Guys 1 and 2 have to do a little "dance" so that they switch places while being blocked from the helper's view.
- **STEP 7:** Lost Guy 2 continues the conversation with the helper. He can tell the helper that he's looking for a particular street or building that isn't too far away. Lost Guy 1 continues to walk along behind the door until he is out of sight.

## THE RESULTS

Your job is to watch carefully from somewhere nearby and see if the helper notices that something weird has just happened. You should debrief your helpful person before you let her go on her way. Let her know that she just participated in a study, and thank her for offering to help the "lost guy." Bring everybody together to shake hands. Ask the helper if she noticed that the lost guy changed after the door passed. Tell her how natural it is for people to not see things in situations like this. Explain the whole "change blindness" concept if she's interested. In the end, thank all of them for their help.

## WHY IT MATTERS

It may have occurred to you that this little "trick" could be used by magicians. You're right. Magicians depend on their audience not noticing when they change something. In order for their "magic" to be believed they use temporary distraction (like that door) to keep you off your toes while they make a switch right in front of you. Change blindness is also a problem for eyewitnesses to a crime. Once we think we've seen someone involved in a crime we are often quite confident about what we saw. But researchers have shown people a video of a crime taking place. In the middle of the video the researchers did something quite similar to what happened here: they switched out the criminal for a completely different person. How many subjects didn't notice this? About 60 percent of them. Findings like this don't provide much support for the accuracy of eyewitness testimony.

# WHY DO YOU REMEMBER CERTAIN THINGS?

## THAT'S DEEP, MAN

**PSYCH CONCEPT:** Levels of Processing
**NAME OF EXPERIMENT:** Depth of Processing and the Retention of Words in Episodic Memory
**ORIGINAL SCIENTIST/RESEARCH:** Fergus I. M. Craik and Endel Tulving (1975)

MEMORY

Our memory is so important. Students certainly have a lot to remember and their grades in school and college depend heavily on their ability to remember. Also, now that there are more middle-aged and older people in the population, new expressions about memory (or the lack of it) are finding their way into our speech. Have you ever heard someone say they are having a "senior moment"?

So why do we forget? Craig and Tulving suggest that one reason we forget is that we don't process what we would like to remember at a deep level. We only process at the surface level. And what exactly does this mean? Well, suppose you heard the word "bacchanalian." Not many people know what that word means. It means to be drunk or to be at a celebration that probably involves drunkenness. If you saw that word in a book you might notice how long it is, or how odd-looking, and you might look up its meaning, but more likely than not you'll skip over it, perhaps hoping to catch the meaning later on or perhaps just hoping that you don't really need to know what the word is in order to understand the larger story. Everybody is in a hurry. So you only process the word at a surface level—you noticed that it was long, that it had two Cs next to each other or that it looks like it has the word "alien" inside it. None of these, however, will help you connect the word to its meaning of drunkenness. So why do you forget you saw the word? Because, truthfully, you didn't take the time to process the word more deeply.

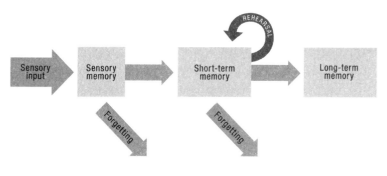

*Progression of memory formation*

Okay, so what would be a "deeper" level of processing for this word? You'd have to look at it and think a bit about it. You could stop for a minute and try to make some guesses about its meaning by looking carefully at the sentences before and after it to see if they provide hints. You could look it up online and learn a little more about its Roman roots. Memory experts are able to memorize words like this because they associate some part of the word with its meaning. In this case, the first three letters of the word "bacchanalian" are "bac," which also stands for "blood alcohol content." This method, called the *keyword method*, helps them to remember the meanings of many words for long periods of time.

That's what you call deep processing.

## THE ORIGINAL EXPERIMENT

Craik and Tulving gave their subjects lists of sixty words (you may have noted that giving subjects lists of words and then asking them to remember the words is pretty darn common in psychological research). The words were not related to each other.

There were several groups of students who were asked to read the words with the anticipation of being tested on them. What was different about the groups was the directions they were given about what to do when they looked at the words. Some subjects were just told to notice whether or not the words were written in all caps or all lowercase. Others were asked to just count the number of vowels in the words. A third group was asked whether or not the word would fit into a fill-in-the-blank sentence. The first two tasks were pretty easily done. The third task required that the person stop for a moment and consider what the word meant before he or she could answer the question.

When these subjects were later asked to recall the words, which one did best? The third group, of course. This group of subjects had to "process" the words at a deeper level than the other two.

Let's do a smaller-scale version of the study by Craik and Tulving that will demonstrate to you and your friends how important deep processing can be to your memory.

## LET'S TRY IT!

You can replicate this study using the basic outline previously provided. Here's what you'll need:

- 3 groups of participants
- List of 15 or so words
- 30 index cards
- Blank paper for participants
- Pencils for participants

Any list of words will do, and fifteen should be enough to make this work. If you'd like, here are fifteen words from the original study.

- Speech
- Brush
- Cheek
- Fence
- Flame
- Flour
- Honey
- Knife
- Sheep
- Copper
- Nurse
- Drill
- Trout
- Bear
- Glass

## WHAT TO DO:

First create 2 separate decks of index cards, each deck containing 15 cards. Each of the 15 cards in deck A should contain one word from your list of 15 in lowercase font. In deck B, you again have 1 word on each of the 15 cards, but this time write half the words in all caps and half the words in all lowercase. Make sure to shuffle the cards within each deck very well.

### GROUP A

- **STEP 1:** Use deck A with this group. Sit your subjects down at a table and tell them that you're going to show them 15 words one at a time on index cards. Give them about 5 seconds maximum to look at the words.
- **STEP 2:** Ask the participants to count the number of vowels in the word and say that number out loud.
- **STEP 3:** When they're done with the task take the index cards away from them. Give them the blank piece of paper and tell them to write down as many words as they can remember.

### GROUP B

- **STEP 1:** Use deck A with this group as well. Sit your subjects down and tell them that you're going to show them 15 words one at a time on index cards.
- **STEP 2:** Ask participants to create a sentence for each word and when they have the sentence they should say it out loud.

- **STEP 3:** When they're done with the task take the index cards away. Give them the blank piece of paper and tell them to write down as many words as they can remember.

### GROUP C
- **STEP 1:** Use deck B with this group (the one with the words in upper and lowercase). Sit the subjects down and tell them that you're going to show them 15 words one at a time on index cards.
- **STEP 2:** Tell them to say out loud whether the word appears in upper or lowercase.
- **STEP 3:** When they're done with the task take the index cards away from them. Give them the blank piece of paper and tell them to write down as many words as they can remember.

## THE RESULTS

You'll probably find that group B—the ones who had to come up with a sentence for the words—will remember more words than the other two groups. That's because the task of coming up with a sentence requires that the person think about the meaning of the word. That's a deeper level of processing than the task you asked the other two groups to do.

## WHY IT MATTERS

If you want to remember more things or if you want to do better on tests, you'll need to process what you're learning at a deeper level than usual. Many students think that copying information from a textbook to their homework means they're studying, and then they're surprised that they don't do well on their tests. But that "studying" was only a surface-level activity. The students didn't really think about what they were learning. Taking the time to really think about what you're learning will really pay off in better grades. One way to do this is to study and then try to explain what you've learned to someone else. If you can't explain it, or the other person doesn't understand it, then you probably need to study that material again. Other tactics: come up with examples for complex ideas or see if you can apply them to your own life. Doing these activities makes the information more likely to "stick" in your brain.

# HOW PHYSICAL WARMTH TRANSLATES TO PSYCHOLOGICAL WARMTH

## I'M WARMING UP TO THE IDEA

**PSYCH CONCEPT:** Psychological Attachment and Embodied Cognition

**NAME OF EXPERIMENT:** The Nature of Love

**ORIGINAL SCIENTIST/RESEARCH:** Harry Harlow (1958)

**NAME OF REPLICATION/EXTENSION:** Experiencing Physical Warmth Promotes Interpersonal Warmth

**REPLICATION SCIENTIST/RESEARCH:** Lawrence E. Williams and John A. Bargh (2008)

COGNITION

Do you remember the study (conducted by Harry Harlow) in which some monkey babies were provided with a "mother" made out of wire and another "mother" also made of wire but covered in cloth? When the monkeys were scared by something they preferred to cling to the cloth mother—even though it was the wire mother that had a milk bottle attached to it. From these studies we learned that babies attach to their mothers for more reasons than just nourishment. Here's something else that was different about the cloth mother: behind her was a 100-watt bulb. So she was both warm and fuzzy.

Okay, so that's monkeys. What does this have to do with you and me? Well, have you ever told a friend that someone you just met isn't very "warm"? Or that somebody gave you the "cold shoulder"? It seems like this idea of warmth is a description we use a lot. Do a web search on the terms "expressions using the word warm" and you'll find quite a list. Since warmth has so many positive associations (such as "sit by a warm fire," "warm and fuzzy," and "a warm welcome"), is it possible that if you experience the physical sensation of warmth when you're near someone you'll like that person more?

Let's find out how important "warmth" really is in our daily lives.

## THE ORIGINAL EXPERIMENT

You could put this idea to the test in a rather straightforward way: put one group of people in a warm room and another group in a cold room and let them interact. Not a bad idea, but all kinds of things could happen when you get people into a room and besides, exactly what would you measure? What is a "warm" reaction and what is a "cold" one?

Williams decided to use coffee instead. Here's how he describes the theory behind this study:

> We hypothesized that mere tactile experiences of physical warmth should activate concepts or feelings of interpersonal warmth. Moreover, this temporarily increased activation of interpersonal warmth concepts should then influence, in an unintentional manner, judgments of and behavior toward other people without one being aware of this influence.

What he actually did is a lot simpler than it sounds from this quote. Here's the scenario:

- You agree to be a participant in a psychological study. You're asked to show up at a specific time in the lobby of a building.
- You show up at the expected time and place and are met by the experimenter who just happens to be holding a clipboard containing paperwork, some textbooks, and a cup of hot coffee. So far everything appears normal.
- The experimenter says that the study will be conducted upstairs, so let's all get on the elevator. Everybody gets on the elevator. Still seems quite ordinary . . .

- While you're riding up the elevator the experimenter says she wants to write down everybody's name on her clipboard, and could you please hold her coffee for a minute while she writes your names down? Gotcha.

You've just been "temperature primed." You took the cup of hot coffee. For other participants the experimenter was holding a cup of iced coffee. Okay, what happened next?

When you arrive on your floor you're told that the study you're about to participate in is a study about "person perception and consumerism," which of course it isn't. You're given this description of Person A:

> Person A is intelligent, skillful, and industrious. Person A is also determined, practical, and cautious.

Based on only this information about the person's personality you are then asked to circle a number for each of ten personality traits for Person A. Some are related to Person A's "warmth" (such as "caring" versus "selfish") and others are just filler items (e.g., "honest" versus "dishonest").

Results? Even with so little information to go on, Williams and Bargh found that the participants who held the hot coffee rated Person A significantly more highly on the "warm" items from the scale.

Hard to believe that an action as minor as holding a cup of hot coffee could affect how you feel about a person you never met? Then let's try it ourselves.

## LET'S TRY IT!

You don't need much in the way of equipment to replicate this study. You can do pretty much what Williams and Bargh did.

Here's what you'll need:

- Cup of hot coffee
- Cup of iced coffee
- Clipboard
- Paperwork
- Textbooks
- 2–4 participants
- Description of Person A
- Writing implements for participants

**WHAT TO DO:**

*GROUP A*
- **STEP 1:** You have your subject show up at the expected time and place. You greet him holding a clipboard containing paperwork, some textbooks, and a cup of hot coffee.
- **STEP 2:** While walking to the study area you make some excuse for needing to write something on your clipboard and kindly ask your participant to hold your hot coffee. Your participant should briefly hold your coffee—anywhere from 15–25 seconds.
- **STEP 3:** Have the participant sit down at a table, and give him the description of Person A. The participant should then rate Person A by circling the numbers on the following scale, which is the one used by Williams and Bargh:

1. Generous **1 2 3 4 5 6 7** Ungenerous
2. Happy **1 2 3 4 5 6 7** Unhappy
3. Good-Natured **1 2 3 4 5 6 7** Irritable
4. Sociable **1 2 3 4 5 6 7** Antisocial
5. Caring **1 2 3 4 5 6 7** Selfish
6. Attractive **1 2 3 4 5 6 7** Unattractive
7. Carefree **1 2 3 4 5 6 7** Serious

8.  Talkative  **1**  **2**  **3**  **4**  **5**  **6**  **7**  Quiet
9.  Strong  **1**  **2**  **3**  **4**  **5**  **6**  **7**  Weak
10. Honest  **1**  **2**  **3**  **4**  **5**  **6**  **7**  Dishonest

### *GROUP B*

- **STEP 1:** You have your subject show up at the expected time and place. You greet her holding a clipboard containing paperwork, some textbooks, and a cup of iced coffee.
- **STEP 2:** While walking to the study area you make some excuse for needing to write something on your clipboard and kindly ask your participant to hold your iced coffee. The participant should briefly hold the iced coffee—anywhere from 15–25 seconds.
- **STEP 3:** Have the participant sit down at a table, and give her the description of Person A. The participant should then rate Person A on the same scale used in group A.

## THE RESULTS

We're only interested in the numbers people circled for the first five questions. Those are the ones that the researchers think will be affected by the "warm/cold" effect. They reversed the items so that higher numbers indicated more warmth. They found that the hot coffee group gave Person A an average of 4.71, while the iced coffee group gave Person A an average of 4.08. This isn't a huge difference, but it is statistically significant.

## WHY IT MATTERS

Physical warmth is important for a child's development. Apparently, the effects of warmth can extend to a lot of different parts of our lives many years later. Advertisers know this as well. That's why they try to associate their products with warm fireplaces, warm cups of hot chocolate, and so on. They're hoping that by doing so you'll "warm up" to their products as well.

# DOES RED MAKE YOU MORE ATTRACTIVE?

## I LOVE YOU IN THAT COLOR!

**PSYCH CONCEPT:** Attractiveness

**NAME OF EXPERIMENT:** Romantic Red: Red Enhances Men's Attraction to Women

**ORIGINAL SCIENTIST/RESEARCH:** Andrew J. Elliot and Daniela Niesta (2008)

COGNITION

Are men more attracted to women wearing red clothes? We all want to look our best, and this is especially true when it comes to romantic relationships. We have theories about the effect of color on attractiveness: red is "hot" while blue is "cool," for example. Wearing red to attract the male of the species has a long history: red lipstick and rouge were worn by women in ancient Egypt. And what happens to your face when you feel in love or when two people are flirting? As these researchers point out:

> The pairing of red and sex in society has a long history that continues to the present. In some of the earliest rituals known to anthropologists, red ochre was used as face and body paint on females to symbolize the emergence of fertility. . . . Red often appears as a symbol of passion, lust, and fertility in ancient mythology and folklore.

Leave it to psychology researchers to gather some hard data on this topic.

## THE ORIGINAL EXPERIMENT

Elliot and Niesta first gathered pictures of attractive women. Researchers are always looking for a little "room for individual interpretation" when they do attractiveness research, so they didn't want photos of extremely beautiful people like movie stars (whose faces are also familiar), but rather pictures of women who would rate, say, a 7 on anyone's 10-point scale. And that's pretty much what you have to do to find the right photo: show lots of them to people until you find one that gets a consistent 7 (to be specific, the researchers used a photo of a woman who scored a 6.8 on a 9-point scale—hey, this is science).

They made the image 4" × 6" and centered it on an 8½" × 11" piece of paper. At first, they changed the background color of the paper. One group saw the picture of the "moderately attractive adult woman" centered on a red piece of paper while the other group saw the picture in the center of a matte white background.

Sure enough, the men rated the attractiveness of the woman they saw on the red paper at about a 7.4 while the woman with the white background was rated about a 6.4. It's interesting to note that women participants did not differ significantly in their assessments of the woman's attractiveness no matter what background she appeared against. The researchers also asked participants to fill out scales to measure whether they thought the woman they saw on the red paper was more intelligent or more kind. They did not find a difference here between the ratings given to the woman surrounded by red or by white.

Elliot and Niesta also used Photoshop to change the color of the shirt in a photo of a moderately attractive woman. When the woman was seen wearing a shirt that was red, she was again seen as more attractive than when the color of the shirt was blue.

This study isn't a hard one to replicate. It would be great if you had some Photoshop photo-editing skills, but I think we can get around that. Let's dive in.

## LET'S TRY IT!

You'll need a photo of a moderately attractive woman. Or you could do a variation on the research and get pictures of men and have your subjects be women. If you'd like to do that, go for it!

For this example I'll stick to pretty much what the researchers did, and you can modify the procedure as you see fit. So, you need to get yourself a photo of a woman. Here are some requirements:

- The woman should be moderately attractive with a simple smile
- The shot should be from the shoulders up
- There should be no one or nothing else in the photo
- Photo should have a plain, white background

Here's what you'll need for this experiment:

- Photo of woman
- 2 groups of participants
- Paper with attractiveness questions printed on it
- Writing implements for participants

### WHAT TO DO:

- **STEP 1:** Go online, search, and download images using the terms "moderately attractive woman isolated." The word "isolated" is what will help you see more images of a person against a white background.
- **STEP 2:** Show the pictures to friends and have them rate her from 1–10. Pick out the woman who is rated between a 6 and a 7.
- **STEP 3:** You need to change the color of the shirt or top that she's wearing. If you have Photoshop or Photoshop Elements and don't yet know how to use them, you can find many tutorials on YouTube by searching on the term "change color of person's clothes." There

also are, however, mobile apps for iOS and Android that will allow you do this color changing. Search on terms like "change color of person's clothes app" and you'll find several free or low-cost apps. Whatever tool you use to change the color of her clothes, you'll need to wind up with two photos that are exactly the same except for that one thing—in one photo she has on a red top and in the other that same top appears blue (or green—the researchers tried several colors, and red always won out in the ratings).

- **STEP 4:** Elliot and Niesta printed out their images on paper but you could use a smartphone to show your participants the pictures.
- **STEP 5:** Print out the questions Elliot and Niesta gave to their participants for your participants to mark. The questions are:

How attractive do you think this person is?

Not at all   **1   2   3   4   5   6   7   8   9**   Extremely

If I were to meet the person in this picture face to face,
I would think she is attractive.

No, definitely not   **1   2   3   4   5   6   7   8   9**   Yes, definitely

Imagine that you are not dating anyone,
and have decided to try computer dating. If you see this
person on a computer dating website, would you ask her out?

No, definitely not   **1   2   3   4   5   6   7   8   9**   Yes, definitely

Imagine that you are going on a date with this person
and you have $100 in your wallet. How much money
would you be likely to spend on your date?

**$0   $10   $20   $30   $40   $50   $60   $70   $80   $90   $100**

## GROUP A: RED SHIRT

- **STEP 1:** When you've got your participants ready, tell them, as Elliot and Niesta did, that you are studying first impressions of the opposite sex. That's not entirely true, but you'll be debriefing them when the study is done.

- **STEP 2:** Show these participants the photo of the woman in the red-colored shirt. You can have the image printed out or available on your cell phone, but always do it the same way each time.
- **STEP 3:** Hand your participant the questions printed out on a piece of paper. Have them answer the questions, and when they are done put the word "red" on the back of the paper. You can then explain what the study is really about.

### GROUP B: BLUE SHIRT

- **STEP 1:** When you've got your participants ready, tell them that you are studying first impressions of the opposite sex. That's not entirely true, but you'll be debriefing them when the study is done.
- **STEP 2:** Show these participants the photo of the woman in a blue-colored shirt. You can have the image printed out or available on your cell phone, but always do it the same way each time.
- **STEP 3:** Hand your participant the questions printed out on a piece of paper. Have them answer the questions, and when they are done put the word "blue" on the back of the paper. You can then explain what the study is really about.

## THE RESULTS

For each participant, add up the first two questions to get an average "attractiveness rating," since the questions are essentially asking the same thing. Average up your answers by group for the other two questions separately. I think you'll find that the woman in the red shirt is rated as more attractive, would be more likely to be asked out on a date, and would have more money spent on her. As you've no doubt noticed, this research is pretty traditional regarding sex roles: men are rating women's attractiveness, they are deciding whether to ask her out on a date, and even estimating how much money they would spend on her. Feel free to make some updates to this research; have women rate men in red and blue shirts. You could also see if colors affect a person's ratings of how likely it is that he or she would be interested in a long-term relationship with the person in the red or blue clothes.

## WHY IT MATTERS

It appears that if you're looking for a romantic partner, wearing red may your best bet. Notice, though, that red is also used in advertisements—red cars and red-colored product packaging. You can be sure that advertisers have tried out their products in different colored packaging in their labs to see which color is perceived most favorably. This happens long before you see the product on the shelves.

# OUR BODIES INFLUENCE US MORE THAN WE THINK

## IS THE CART BEFORE THE HORSE? OR THE TAIL WAGGING THE DOG?

**PSYCH CONCEPT:** Emotions

**NAME OF EXPERIMENT:** Duchenne Smile, Emotional Experience, and Autonomic Reactivity: A Test of the Facial Feedback Hypothesis

**ORIGINAL SCIENTIST/RESEARCH:** Robert Soussignan (2002)

EMOTIONS

Do you smile because you're happy—or are you happy because you're smiling? Most of us, of course, think that the first of these is correct: we feel an emotion and then we express it through out bodies. But think about it. Haven't you ever told a friend who's feeling down to get off their feet and go somewhere else, have fun, and distract themselves from whatever is bothering them? We do this because we know that changing your body position—getting up, moving around, seeing new things—can change how we feel on the inside.

So as weird as "you're happy because you smile" might sound at first, there may actually be something to it. There's still a bit of controversy around the idea, so let's take a look at how psychologists study this and then you'll see how you too can test this out with an odd but fun little experiment.

*Facial changes triggering emotion*

## THE ORIGINAL EXPERIMENT

What we're looking at here is called the "facial feedback hypothesis," which is the idea that you judge how funny something is by how closely the muscles in your face approach a smile. Weird, I know.

So how do we get someone to smile without them knowing they're doing it? Soussignan came up with the idea of telling subjects that they were participating in research to help the physically challenged. Here's what subjects were told:

> This research is part of a project on physically handicapped persons who are unable to use their hands to exercise control over their environment. However, one may expect that training would make these persons able to use other parts of their body (mouth, feet) in order to do daily routine psychomotor or cognitive tasks. The tasks we would like you to perform aim specifically at assessing your reactions to a particular pencil-holding technique with the mouth. . . . Several techniques of pencil holding will be compared . . . you will also have to hold the pencil with the mouth, and to direct it toward the television facing you.

There were four ways of holding the pencil in the mouth; the last one was the one that put the facial muscles into the correct position for a smile. Get yourself a pencil and give these a try:

1. Hold the pencil between the teeth; open the lips slightly without touching the pencil
2. Tightly hold the pencil with the lips without touching it with the teeth
3. Hold the pencil with the teeth, avoid any contact of the lips, and mimic the experimenter (who pulled his lips back just a little)

4. Hold the pencil with the teeth, avoid any contact of the lips, and mimic the experimenter (who pulled his lips back AND raised his cheeks)

The last way of holding the pencil will create a smile on your face—without anyone asking you to directly smile.

Now how do you show participants something that's funny in order to find out if the people in the fourth condition (who are already smiling) thought it was funnier than the people in the other groups? Soussignan simply placed a TV in front of them and showed them short videos that they had selected to be "more or less pleasant and more or less funny." They were to point the pencil at the part of the screen they were paying the most attention to.

None of the participants in this study figured out that the researchers were actually looking to see if the facial feedback hypothesis was being tested. Sure enough, the videos were reported as being funniest by those holding the pencil in a way that approximates a smile.

## LET'S TRY IT!

You could replicate this study using just the last two ways of holding the pencil and some moderately funny video:

### WHAT TO DO:
- **STEP 1:** Use Soussignan's cover story of how you're doing research on the best way for physically challenged individuals to hold a pencil to operate things around them in the house. As always, you'll want to debrief your participants later about what you're really studying.
- **STEP 2:** Ask one group of participants to sit down about 3 feet in front of a TV and hold a pencil between the teeth with the lips only slightly pulled back.

- **STEP 3:** Ask your other group of participants to sit about 3 feet in front of a TV and hold a pencil between their teeth with the lips slightly pulled and the cheeks raised.
- **STEP 4:** Show each person (though you could do this in groups) one video on your TV of about 3 minutes in length. You don't want the video to be too funny or your participants will drop their pencils or catch on to what you're doing. (There are plenty of cat videos on the web. You could try to find a compilation that is pleasant and about 3 minutes in length.)
- **STEP 5:** Just before you play the video, ask your participants to point the pencil at whatever on the screen is holding their attention.
- **STEP 6:** Begin the video.
- **STEP 7:** When the video is over, have these two questions typed out on paper and ask each person to circle a number on each scale:

How difficult was it to hold the pencil in this way?

Not at all difficult   **1**   **2**   **3**   **4**   **5**   **6**   **7**   **8**   **9**   **10**   Very difficult

How did you react to the video clip?

Not at all funny   **1**   **2**   **3**   **4**   **5**   **6**   **7**   **8**   **9**   **10**   Very funny

- **STEP 8:** Thank them for their participation. When each person or each group is done you can debrief them and tell them a little about the "facial feedback hypothesis."

## THE RESULTS

You're really only interested in their answers to the second question about their reaction to the video clip. If the "facial feedback hypothesis" is correct, the group holding the pencil with the cheeks raised should rate the video, on average, as funnier than the other group. Not all studies have found this though, so you'll be on the "cutting edge" of the controversy.

## WHY IT MATTERS

It's important to realize that influence goes both ways—our minds influence our bodies and our bodies provide feedback to our minds that help us understand ourselves. If you find yourself laughing (or crying) more forcefully than you anticipated, you will judge what your emotion is based on this feedback from your body. Many comedians believe that one reason why words that have the hard "k" sound in them are funny (like chicken and quack) is because the hard "k" puts your facial muscles in the smiling position. Something to think about.

# WHEN TRYING TO LOOK GOOD LOOKS BAD

## *MY WHAT BIG WORDS YOU HAVE!*

**PSYCH CONCEPT:** Intelligence/Influence

**NAME OF EXPERIMENT:** Consequences of Erudite Vernacular Utilized Irrespective of Necessity: Problems with Using Long Words Needlessly

**ORIGINAL SCIENTIST/RESEARCH:** Daniel Oppenheimer (2006)

SOCIAL

At some point or another you're going to have to write an e-mail to impress someone. Perhaps you'll be writing a cover letter for a job or a written assignment for school or a note to your boss. You'll be tempted to use words that are more formal and certainly bigger than words you typically use. The research we're going to describe and carry out here tested this out and the conclusion is clear: don't do it. You'll only make your words harder to read and understand, and that results in your reader judging you as less intelligent than the person who can write in a more "down to earth" way. Let's find out how psychology went about studying this.

## THE ORIGINAL EXPERIMENT

To conduct a study on the effect of big words on impressions of intelligence, you're going to need something for your participants to read and judge. Since Daniel Oppenheimer is a professor at Stanford University, he decided to use something he was quite familiar with: essays written by college seniors regarding why they wanted to go to graduate school for a degree in English literature. Oppenheimer used paragraphs of about 75–100 words long.

You want your participants to all be reading essentially the same paragraph, but you need some of these paragraphs to contain big words. Oppenheimer's solution was elegant: he took a paragraph of relatively easy-to-read text and created a moderately difficult version of it by "replacing every third noun, verb, and adjective with its longest entry in the Microsoft Word 2000 thesaurus." He then created a highly complex version of the paragraph by replacing not only every third noun, verb, and adjective with its longer equivalent, but by replacing every single noun, verb, and adjective with a longer word.

Let's look at an example. Oppenheimer started with this relatively easy-to-understand paragraph:

I want to go to Graduate School so that I can learn to know literature well. I want to explore the shape and the meaning of the novel and its literary antecedents. I want to understand what the novel has meant in different literary periods, and what it is likely to become. I want to explore its different forms, realism, naturalism, and other modes, and the Victorian and Modernist consciousness as they are revealed.

By replacing every third noun, verb, and adjective, it became this moderately difficult paragraph:

I want to go to Graduate School so that I can learn to recognize literature well. I want to explore the character and the meaning of the novel and its literary antecedents. I desire to understand what the novel has represented in different literary periods, and what it is likely to become. I desire to explore its different manners, realism, naturalism and other modes, and the Victorian and Modernist consciousness as they are revealed.

And by replacing all nouns, verbs, and adjectives, it became this highly complex paragraph:

> I desire to go to Graduate School so that I can learn to recognize literature satisfactorily. I want to investigate the character and the connotation of the narrative and its literary antecedents. I desire to comprehend what the narrative has represented in numerous literary periods, and what it is expected to become. I desire to investigate its numerous manners, realism, naturalism, and other approaches, and the Victorian and Modernist consciousness as they are discovered.

Participants read the paragraphs and decide whether or not to accept the person into graduate school and rate their confidence on this decision.

The result? Those very intelligent-sounding complex essays received few acceptances and less confidence. Let's see if we can replicate this.

## LET'S TRY IT!

First, let's agree that you don't have to "reinvent the wheel." If you want to use the paragraphs Oppenheimer did, then go right ahead. But you could place this study in another situation: how about people applying for a job? Here's what you'll need:

- 3 groups of participants
- Example of well-written cover letter

You can find two paragraphs of a well-written cover letter on the Internet. You don't want a letter that's perfect—just a nicely written cover letter for an ordinary job like a salesperson.

## WHAT TO DO:

- **STEP 1:** As Oppenheimer did, identify the nouns, verbs, and adjectives in every sentence in the paragraphs and then use your computer's built-in thesaurus or head over to www.thesaurus.com to find synonyms. Create a moderately complex version by replacing every third such word with a word that's longer but means the same thing.

- **STEP 2:** Next create a highly complex version by replacing every single noun, verb, and adjective with a longer, complicated word from the thesaurus. Doing this kind of replacing may require a little "massaging" of the text just to make sure that the new words fit in well with the rest of the sentence, but make as few changes as possible to the other words.

### GROUP A

- **STEP 1:** Give this group the cover letter paragraphs just as you found them on the web. Tell them you're doing research on the hiring process and ask them to read the paragraphs.

- **STEP 2:** After they read the paragraphs have all the participants circle their answers to these two questions:

Would you hire this person for the job? **Yes** or **No**

How confident are you in this decision?

–7  –6  –5  –4  –3  –2  –1  0  1  2  3  4  5  6  7

Not at all confident                                    Very confident

### GROUP B

- **STEP 1:** Give this group the moderately complex paragraphs that were created from the original.

- **STEP 2:** Ask the participants to circle their answers to the same questions you gave to group A.

### GROUP C

- **STEP 1:** Give this group the highly complex paragraphs you created.
- **STEP 2:** Ask the participants to circle their answers to the same questions you gave to group A.

## THE RESULTS

Oppenheimer put the two questions together in a unique way: if a person circled Yes, the response was given a +1. If a person circled No, the response was marked as a –1. Then he multiplied this number times the number the person circled on the confidence scale. Why? Well, let's say you think the person should not be hired (No = –1) and you're really confident about this (7). Your final rating would calculate out as a –7. On the other hand, if you said Yes to hire the person (+1) and that you were very confident about this decision too (+7), then your rating would be a +7. So higher numbers mean greater confidence in the person.

You'll probably find what Oppenheimer did: the fictional person who wrote the original essay without the big words was viewed most positively.

## WHY IT MATTERS

This study has some clear implications: don't try to come off as intelligent in your writing. Think through your cover letter or your application to school carefully, but then don't mess it up with flowery long words. As one well-known psychologist (Daryl Bem) once said, "the first step toward clarity is writing simply." Oh yes, and some other guy (Albert Einstein) said, "If you can't explain it simply, you don't understand it well enough."

# BRAIN IMAGES AND PERSUASION

## SEE? A PICTURE OF A BRAIN—NOW DO YOU BELIEVE ME?

**PSYCH CONCEPT:** Persuasion/Influence

**NAME OF EXPERIMENT:** Seeing Is Believing: The Effect of Brain Images on Judgments of Scientific Reasoning

**ORIGINAL SCIENTIST/RESEARCH:** David P. McCabe and Alan D. Castel (2008)

**NAME OF REPLICATION/EXTENSION:** On the (Non)Persuasive Power of a Brain Image

**REPLICATION SCIENTIST/RESEARCH:** Robert B. Michael, Eryn J. Newman, Matti Vuorre, Geoff Cumming, and Maryanne Garry (2013)

SOCIAL

In this chapter we're going to do a "psych smackdown." We'll try to resolve an argument among researchers. As you can imagine, when researchers argue it's not a pretty sight. One thing they're arguing about is how easily the general public can be persuaded to think that a scientific finding is credible when it really isn't.

As you cruise around the web, you have no doubt seen articles that include colorful and impressive pictures of the brain. These pictures typically come from either MRI (magnetic resonance imaging) or PET (positron emission tomography) brain scans. They look very "scientific." So if I were a journalist and I found a dubious study that probably was done poorly but it's an interesting topic (and I could probably get you to click on it), could I make you believe it was good scientific research if I just included a picture of a brain scan on the page?

Some researchers say yes—we are easily persuaded simply by pictures of brains. Others, including Michael et al., say no, you're not. You're going to settle the argument.

## THE ORIGINAL EXPERIMENT

McCabe and Castel did the original study, so let's replicate what they did. It's pretty straightforward. They showed participants an article they found on the web that described research claiming that brain scans could be used as lie detectors. The idea sounds like it could work: when you're making up a lie your brain has to work harder than when you simply tell the truth. Thus, if we put you into an fMRI (Functional Magnetic Resonance Imager) and ask you to lie about something, and then we see that your frontal lobe (the lobe that does all your complex thinking) is very active, it means that you're probably trying to come up with a lie.

Actually the research is a little suspect. The study was done using volunteers who were asked to lie while having the brain scan, so we're not talking about real criminals here. Also, your frontal lobe is always busy thinking about one thing or another. In this case it got busy when these people were trying to come up with a good lie. In real life, wouldn't it also get busy when an innocent person is trying very hard to put together the details of what they saw?

You can read the article here: http://news.bbc.co.uk/2/hi/uk_news/4268260.stm. So the question is this: if you read this article, would a picture of a brain scan on the page influence you to believe the study was credible?

## LET'S TRY IT!

This study is not hard to replicate. Here's what you'll need:

- 2 groups of participants
- Article of about 500 words that describes a piece of research that is perhaps a little controversial or at least a little difficult to understand. Since the article McCabe and Castel used is still available online, you could even use that one.
- Image of an fMRI brain scan. These are easy to find. Just do a search on "fmri brain scan" and download a colorful image of a brain.

### WHAT TO DO:
- **STEP 1:** Copy the title and the text of the article and save it to your computer.
- **STEP 2:** Underneath the article, at the bottom of the page, type in this question: Do you agree or disagree with the article's conclusion that _____? Instead of a blank line type in whatever your article concludes. In this case it would be that brain scans can be used to detect lies. Below the question put a 1 to 10 scale with "strongly disagree" near the 1 and "strongly agree" near the 10.
- **STEP 3:** Make a copy of this page and in this version, insert your image of an fMRI brain scan at the top right corner of the page next to the title. Don't make the image too large or your participants might suspect what you're doing.

### GROUP A
- **STEP 1:** Tell the participants in this group that you're doing some research on neuroscience. Ask them to read the article (the one without the picture of the brain scan).
- **STEP 2:** Ask participants in this group to answer the question at the bottom. That's it. Take the paper from them and do a little debriefing—tell them what you're actually looking at (the

persuasiveness of a brain image). Ask them not to tell anyone else about your study and that you'll be happy to let them know what you find out.

### GROUP B

- **STEP 1:** Give the participants in this group the article that includes the picture of the brain scan.
- **STEP 2:** Ask participants in this group to answer the same questions as group A. Give them the same instructions as you did for group A.

## THE RESULTS

Since this is a "smackdown" we don't really know for sure how this is going to come out. If McCabe and Castel are correct, you will find higher numbers on your agree/disagree scale on the page that includes the brain scan image. If Michael et al. are correct you won't find a difference at all between the two groups. You'll be participating in a key component of the scientific process (one that doesn't get done often enough): a replication intended to find out if we can have confidence in the results of the original study.

## WHY IT MATTERS

The results of scientific articles are reported very often in the popular press and it's important that we know whether we can believe what we read. Remember that not all research is good research and that journalists are often not so interested in whether you know the truth. They're interested in getting you to click on the article title and visit their webpage. If a picture of a brain will get you to do that, then they're going to use it to persuade you. Let's hope that Michael et al. are correct—you are not so easily persuaded.

# OUR BRAINS LOVE CURIOSITY

## *FIVE REASONS WHY YOU'LL READ THIS ENTRY FIRST!*

**PSYCH CONCEPT:** Neuroscience of Motivation/Persuasion

**NAME OF EXPERIMENT:** The Wick in the Candle of Learning: Epistemic Curiosity Activates Reward Circuitry and Enhances Memory

**ORIGINAL SCIENTIST/RESEARCH:** Min Jeong Kang, Ming Hsu, Ian M. Krajbich, George Loewenstein, Samuel M. McClure, Joseph Tao-yi Wang, and Colin F. Camerer (2009)

SOCIAL

Neuroscience is one of the most popular areas in psychology right now. Part of the reason is that with all the new brain scanning techniques available (MRI, fMRI, and PET) we're finally able to "look inside the black box" of your brain to see what's going on in there. One human tendency researchers have examined is our tendency to be curious. Have you ever been working on your computer and a Facebook or Twitter notification pops up that includes a really interesting question? I'll bet you couldn't resist. You stopped what you were doing to find out the answer.

Kang et al. decided to see what was going on inside our brains when our curiosity is piqued. I'm going to guess you don't happen to have an fMRI scanner around your house, so we won't be able to replicate that part of their study, but we can still put their findings to the test. And I'll bet that along the way you'll learn something very useful for your daily life.

# THE ORIGINAL EXPERIMENT

Kang et. al put participants into an fMRI scanner and presented them with trivia questions. Some of these questions had previously been rated as questions that made people really curious to find out the answer. Other questions were only a little bit interesting.

Here are some of the "high curiosity" questions they used:

- What book is the most shoplifted book in the world? (The Bible)
- What snack food is an ingredient in the explosive dynamite? (Peanuts)
- What breed of dog is the only animal whose evidence is admissible in American courts? (Bloodhound)
- What is the only country in the world where women dominate the government? (Belgium)
- What is the only type of animal besides a human that can get a sunburn? (Pig)

Here are some "low curiosity" questions:

- How long were Jerry Seinfeld and his pals sentenced in the series finale? (One year)
- Which school has the most students over age twenty-five according to *U.S. News*? (University of Phoenix)
- What city is referred to as the "Pittsburgh of the South"? (Birmingham, AL)
- What president has three As in his first name where each has a different sound? (Abraham Lincoln)
- Which sports athlete has appeared in McDonald's, Nike, and Hanes advertisements? (Michael Jordan)

Kang found that the following regions of the brain became active when participants were asked the high-curiosity questions:

- Caudate Nucleus
- Bilateral Prefrontal Cortex
- Parahippocampal Gyri
- Putamen
- Globus Pallidus

Now, unless you're a brain scientist (and I'm not one either) you may not know what those regions of the brain do. As it turns out, they're related to both the reward and memory centers of the brain. So it appears that our brains reward us when we find the answer to really interesting questions. Kang also found that when the answer is contrary to what we originally thought, these brain regions that are involved in memory "kick in" to help us remember this new information.

Let's try this out for ourselves.

## LET'S TRY IT!

Pretty much every time you go to a website you see the results of this study at work. This idea that you can be "pulled in" by curiosity-inducing headlines is put to very good use by anyone who is trying to induce you to come to their website. Have you ever seen a post titled something like this: "This dog found his way home and you will not believe what happens next!" or "5 things you need to do today to avoid getting sick"? These types of titles attempt to instill a "curiosity itch" or a "knowledge gap," and you just have to know the answer.

The second part of Kang's study, which didn't use the fMRI, can be replicated. What we'll do is plan out a fake website—one that contains "curiosity-inducing" headlines as well as headlines that don't induce curiosity. Which ones will people probably click on?

Here is what you'll need:

- Blank background for our fake website. You could use a blank page in your word processor, but a poster board of about 22" × 28" might be more fun.
- 5 articles that have "curiosity-inducing" titles and 5 that don't.
- Participants

**WHAT TO DO:**

- **STEP 1:** You could use titles from articles found on sites like www .buzzfeed.com, www.upworthy.com, or www.vox.com, which are sites that really make use of this strategy. Find ten articles that you like.
- **STEP 2:** Pick five of these articles and create alternate headlines that don't induce much curiosity. For example, here's an actual "curiosity-inducing" title: "29 Photos That Prove Both America and Britain Have Ruined Food." You really want to find out what those foods are, don't you? An alternate, boring title might be this: "Differences Between American and British Food."
- **STEP 3:** Put the ten titles (five have curiosity-inducing titles and five don't) on your blank word processor page or on your poster board. Increase the font size and arrange the titles on the page so it looks like you're building a mockup of a webpage. Most webpages also contain images, of course, but we're only interested in the effect of titles on curiosity; don't include images.
- **STEP 4:** You won't need two groups of participants for this study. You'll be showing your "website mockup" to all your subjects one at a time.
- **STEP 5:** Show the page or poster board to a participant and say that you want her feedback on which five of the ten articles she would probably click on if this were a real site.
- **STEP 6:** If you're doing this on poster board you could give your participants five chips each and ask them to place a chip next to

*Our Brains Love Curiosity*

each of the five articles they would click on (that's the approach Kang used). If you did this on a computer you could bold the text of the titles they select.

- **STEP 7:** That's it. Make sure to debrief your participants about what exactly you were looking for in your study.

## THE RESULTS

I think you'll find that your participants will select the "curiosity-inducing" titles. As Kang et al. found using an fMRI, these kinds of titles are just too hard to resist.

## WHY IT MATTERS

Like it or not, you are the target of influence every single day. You should be aware that advertisers are using this "curiosity effect" to get you to click. And, since you're probably aware that your clicking behavior is being tracked, you're going to be presented with more of the kind of things you click on. Take control of this. Resist the urge to click on things that sound interesting but that are really not important to you. Or turn off your notifications when you need to get work done.

# HOW YOUR BEHAVIOR IS SHAPED

## *I CAN GET YOU TO DO PRETTY MUCH WHATEVER I WANT*

**PSYCH CONCEPT:** Behaviorism/Operant Conditioning
**NAME OF EXPERIMENT:** "Superstition" in the Pigeon
**ORIGINAL SCIENTIST/RESEARCH:** B. F. Skinner (1948)

**LEARNING**

When asked about things that make you think about the field of psychology most people would say Pavlov's dogs, Freud himself, or the vase/faces illusion. But high on that list is also mice in mazes and pigeons in "Skinner boxes." Burhuss Frederic Skinner did indeed carry out a lot of research using pigeons, and his findings have stood the test of time. They still deserve a lot of respect.

What tends to put people off about Skinner is that when it comes to explaining why we do what we do, he didn't give that much weight to our thoughts. He preferred to focus on reinforcers from our environment. Skinner would say that you do what you do largely because you've been reinforced for doing that behavior in the past (with candy, or attention

*An example of a Skinner box*

from others). I'm going to guess that you don't have any pet pigeons around the house that you can try this on. So let's use humans and do something creative with this idea of conditioning (or shaping) their behavior.

# THE ORIGINAL EXPERIMENT

In one of his most famous studies Skinner showed how even the idea of a "superstition"—which we think of as something uniquely human—could be created in a pigeon. Typically, Skinner could get pigeons to perform very specific behaviors, like pecking a bar or raising their heads up as high as they could or even playing Ping-Pong by rewarding them when they exhibited small behaviors that approximated the larger behavior he wanted them to perform. This method became known as the method of successive approximations, or more simply as "shaping."

Then he decided to drop a food pellet into the box at random times to see if he could create what looked like superstitious behavior. Sure enough, after only a little while the pigeons started to do whatever they happened to be doing when the pellet dropped into the box. Skinner calls this "conditioning." Here's how he described what happened:

> One bird was conditioned to turn counter-clockwise about the cage, making two or three turns between reinforcements. Another repeatedly thrust its head into one of the upper corners of the cage. A third developed a 'tossing' response, as if placing its head beneath an invisible bar and lifting it repeatedly.

So maybe even superstitious behavior, which we think of as a uniquely human "quirk," is just another example of reinforcement at work.

I'm going to guess that you don't have any pet pigeons around the house that we can experiment on. So let's use humans. We'll see if we can "shape" them to do what we want.

**LET'S TRY IT!**

Here's what you'll need for the equipment:

- Participants
- Musical keyboard

Yup. That's all. You don't even have to know how to play the piano.

**WHAT TO DO:**

- **STEP 1:** Decide what you'd like your participants to do when they enter whatever room you decide to conduct your study in. Here's an example: you want your participant to enter the room, go over to a desk, open a drawer, take out a pencil and paper (which you've previously put there), and write their name on the paper with the pencil. If you do this at home you could decide that you'd like your participants to go into the kitchen, open the cabinet, pull out a mug, then open the refrigerator and get out the milk and pour the milk into the mug. Get the idea? Be creative.
- **STEP 2:** Tell your participants that at the start you're going to play a low note on the keyboard until they do a series of behaviors that you want them to do. Assure them that you won't ask them to do anything embarrassing.
- **STEP 3:** Tell them to just start doing things (Skinner would call these random behaviors "operants") and that as they get closer to doing what you want them to do you're going to play higher notes on the keyboard. When they have done everything you want, you'll play the highest note on the keyboard and shout "Yes!"
- **STEP 4:** Say "Begin."
- **STEP 5:** Start with a low note—either hold it down or tap it repeatedly.
- **STEP 6:** Play higher notes as your participants get closer to doing the first behavior you want (such as standing near the desk or going

How Your Behavior Is Shaped

into the kitchen). Slowly go higher each time they do something that is slightly closer to what you want.

- **STEP 7:** You may have to go from a high note back to a lower one if they move toward the refrigerator but then start to walk away from it. They'll get the message. Don't say anything. Don't give them hints like smiles or pointing.

## THE RESULTS

It might take a little while, but you'll be surprised how quickly you get the participants to do exactly what you want. You will have shaped a person's behavior using no words at all—just sounds. You could throw them a candy, but that would get old (and expensive). A tone on the piano will work. Others have used just clapping their hands as the reinforcer.

## WHY IT MATTERS

Some people didn't like Skinner's work because they thought he was saying that humans don't think—that we're just robots. That is not at all what he was saying. He was trying to get us to realize that there are external influences on our behavior and that we didn't need to create complex theories to explain behavior and to make our society a better place. His is one of the most practical of psychological theories. Shaping is used today to train animals at home and in the circus, to help children learn at school, to get children with autism to be more social, and to help people overcome their phobias.

# HOW DOES CREATIVITY REALLY WORK?

## *YOU'RE MORE CREATIVE THAN YOU THINK*

**PSYCH CONCEPT:** Creativity

**NAME OF EXPERIMENT:** The Green Eggs and Ham Hypothesis: How Constraints Facilitate Creativity

**ORIGINAL SCIENTIST/RESEARCH:** Catrinel Haught-Tromp (2016)

COGNITION

Most people have heard of or read the famous children's book *Green Eggs and Ham* (if you haven't then go get it—it's an extremely quick read). What you may not know is that the author (Theodor Geisel, also known as "Dr. Seuss") wrote the book after his publisher dared him to write a children's book using the same fifty words or less. It's a fun, creative little book that has been wildly successful.

We usually think that creativity bursts out of nowhere and only when writers, composers, or artists are allowed as much time as they need to let their minds run free. Actually, that doesn't appear to be the case. Many famous musical works were written when the composers were told that the song or symphony had to be completed in very little time. That's a constraint. Have you ever been really frustrated at not being able to do something because you didn't have the "right" tools and then you surprised yourself by coming up with a really creative solution?

What psychologists have found is that, as Theodor Geisel discovered, sometimes we can be most creative not when we let our minds run free, but when we have the most constraints placed on us. Let's test this out.

# THE ORIGINAL EXPERIMENT

Researcher Haught-Tromp conducted a fun study that I think you'll enjoy replicating. She asked her participants to write a message inside a greeting card. It had to be two lines long and of course it had to rhyme. The subjects were:

- Happy Birthday
- Thank You
- Good Luck
- I'm Sorry

- Happy New Year
- Congratulations
- Feel Better
- I Love You

For some of her subjects she made the task of writing the message even harder: they had to first write down any concrete noun that came to mind (words like "sun," "chair," "book," etc.). Then they had to use those nouns in their rhymes. Can you imagine creating a two-line rhyme using the word "chair"? Her other subjects didn't have this additional constraint. They could use whatever words came to mind to create the rhyme.

Guess who came up with the more creative greeting card messages? Like Dr. Seuss, it was the people who were given a challenge—the ones who had to use those concrete nouns in their rhymes.

Here's an example of a rhyme in which the person had to incorporate the word "feather" into a Feel Better card:

No matter what storms you may weather, just remember, bad days come and go like a feather.

Not bad. Certainly better than this message, which was written by someone who was under no constraints:

Happy Birthday to you all, I hope you have a ball.

## LET'S TRY IT!

You can do a very direct replication of this study. You don't even need any equipment (aside from paper and pens or pencils). And it'll be fun for everyone.

- 2 groups of participants
- 2 friends to read and judge greetings
- Paper
- Writing implements

You'll need a control group and an experimental group and two friends who agree to read all the greeting card messages and give their judgment on how creative the greetings are. Let's do it.

### WHAT TO DO:

#### GROUP A: UNCONSTRAINED GROUP

- **STEP 1:** Your participants can create their rhymes alone or in groups. It's probably better if they're alone because they won't talk to each other and potentially "steal" ideas. If you do this in a group format just ask them not to talk out loud about their ideas.
- **STEP 2:** Use the eight greeting card topics listed earlier in this chapter. Write them on a piece of paper and provide everyone with a blank piece of paper and a pencil or pen.
- **STEP 3:** Ask this group to write a greeting card message that is two lines long and that rhymes. Each group member should write one message for each of the eight topics (you certainly could use fewer topics if you'd like).
- **STEP 4:** Haught-Tromp gave her subjects as much time as they wanted to do the task, but when your participants are done creating the rhymes they should let you know. Write a *U* on each paper

in the upper right corner so you'll know that this person was in the "Unconstrained" group.

- **STEP 5:** Thank them for their time, explain what the study was about, and ask them not to tell anyone until you're done with your study.

### GROUP B: CONSTRAINED GROUP

- **STEP 1:** Your participants can create their rhymes alone or in groups. It's probably better if they're alone because they won't talk to each other and potentially "steal" ideas. If you do this in a group format just ask them not to talk out loud about their ideas.
- **STEP 2:** Provide everyone with a blank piece of paper and a pencil or pen. Before you have them begin, give the same instructions that Haught-Tromp gave this group: they are to write down the first four concrete nouns that pop into their heads. They'll probably come up with objects they see in the room, like chair, window, light, and cup.
- **STEP 3:** Use the same eight greeting card topics listed earlier in this chapter. Write them on a piece of paper.
- **STEP 4:** Tell the participants that they have to use any of their four nouns in their rhymes.
- **STEP 5:** Give the participants as much time as they want to do the task, but when they're done creating the rhymes they should let you know. When they're done write a *C* (for "constrained") at the top of each page. Thank and debrief as for the first group.

## THE RESULTS

So how are you going to judge the creativity of their rhymes? You can do what Haught-Tromp and other creativity researchers do. Type out the rhymes on a separate piece of paper (so that handwriting isn't a problem) and give them to two people who agree to rate each one on this 10-point scale:

Not at all creative   **1   2   3   4   5   6   7   8   9   10**   Very creative

Creativity raters typically work separately from each other and then their ratings for each rhyme are combined.

See if you find what Haught-Tromp found: the rhymes written when people had to use their concrete words are more unique and imaginative.

## WHY IT MATTERS

We tend to stereotype "creative people" as somehow being different from most of us. Perhaps their hair is wild. We think what they do is mysterious. That's not always the case. Don't think that you're not a creative person because you can't draw, paint, or sing. Creativity takes many forms and it occurs in many different situations in which people had to follow certain rules or time constraints. Computer programmers have come up with some pretty creative solutions when they had to tackle tough programming problems. And if you want to see lots of examples of everyday people coming up with creative solutions to problems, check out www.thereifixedit.com.

# HOW SUPERSTITIONS REALLY WORK

## *A HOLE IN ONE! KNOCK ON WOOD!*

**PSYCH CONCEPT:** Superstition/Critical Thinking

**NAME OF EXPERIMENT:** Keep Your Fingers Crossed! How Superstition Improves Performance

**ORIGINAL SCIENTIST/RESEARCH:** Lysann Damisch, Barbara Stoberock, and Thomas Mussweiler (2010)

COGNITION

Do you have any superstitions? I own a black cat so you can count me out of this—although I do admit to "knocking on wood" on more than a few occasions. But many of us carry around something we think is lucky on our key chains or perhaps in our cars that we hope will keep away car accidents. Many sports professionals have superstitions or have "ritual behaviors" they do before or during a game. Perhaps not surprisingly, the less control you have over your performance (a sports game for example), the more likely you are to have some kind of "lucky charm."

Many scientists would say that there's a "confirmation bias" going on here. That is, when something goes right (you hit a home run or win a game of soccer) and you have your lucky charm on you, you attribute some of your success to the charm. But when things don't go well when you had the charm on you, you don't tend to blame your lucky charm.

But Damisch, Stoberock, and Mussweiler wanted to find out exactly what's going on in your head when you think you have luck on your side. Let's give it a shot and see what we learn.

## THE ORIGINAL EXPERIMENT

Damisch et al. did a bunch of studies on superstitions, one of which involved asking people to come to the lab and bring with them some lucky charm they owned (like a rabbit's foot or a "lucky" medal). They had the participants work on either anagram tasks or a memory task (similar to the Concentration memory game). But for some participants they took away the lucky charm during the task (saying that they wanted to take a picture of it in another room). Those participants wound up doing worse on the memory games.

Why did they do worse? Was it bad luck to have their charm taken away? Well, Damisch et al. had a different explanation. Just before participants attempted the task, Damisch asked them how well they thought they would do. Turns out, when you don't have your lucky charm with you, you expect to not do very well. And you don't. Your self-efficacy for the task (your sense of your ability to do well on it) decreases, and you don't do well as a result. You might call this a self-fulfilling prophesy.

Let's replicate the more fun part of their study. It involves golfing.

## LET'S TRY IT!

Have you ever putted a golf ball into the hole from about 5 feet away? Harder than you think (unless you golf a great deal). Here's what you'll need to test out this idea about superstition the way Damisch did:

- Putting green. If you have a golf course near you that would be great, but if not, then buy an inexpensive golf putting mat, preferably one that has an incline at the end of the mat that leads to the hole.
- Golf ball and putter
- 2 groups of participants—at least 10 per group, or 20 total should be enough. (A carefully controlled psychological study would have at

least 30 participants per group, but rounding up 60 participants for your study might be a little challenging.)

- This question, which you can either present to people on paper or ask out loud: How well do you think you're going to do?

Not well at all **1 2 3 4 5 6 7 8 9 10** Very well

## WHAT TO DO:

### GROUP A

- **STEP 1:** Tell your participants you're doing a psychological study. It involves them doing a golf putting task. They'll look at you strangely. Tell them you'll explain later. If they tell you they've never played golf, tell them it doesn't matter.
- **STEP 2:** Stand participants in front of the golf mat (or about 5 feet away from the actual hole) and hand them the putter. You hold on to the ball for a moment.
- **STEP 3:** Tell them they have ten chances to get the ball in the hole.
- **STEP 4:** Before you hand them the golf ball say this : "Here's the ball that everybody has been using so far." Then hand them the ball.
- **STEP 5:** Just before they start their first putt ask them the question about doing well, or have them circle a number from 1 to 10 if you've written the scale on a piece of paper. Make sure you write down next to their name that the person is in group A (the no superstition group) so you know later which group the person was in.
- **STEP 6:** Let them take their ten putts. If they get it in the hole right away that may mean that in future trials you may want to move your participants a little farther back. But in any case, write down next to each name how many shots it took to get the ball into the hole. If a participant doesn't succeed, just put a 10 next to that person's name. If a participant gets the ball in the hole before 10, write down the number of shots it took and let them use their remaining shots if they want to.

***GROUP B***

Follow all same steps as you did for group A, except for step 4. Here's what you do for step 4:

- **STEP 4:** Before you hand them the golf ball say this, "Here's your ball. So far it has turned out to be a lucky ball." Then blow on the ball before you hand it to them just to heighten this "superstition-activating" effect.

## THE RESULTS

Average up the "confidence" scores and I'll bet you'll find that your "superstition activated" participants are more confident before they take their shots and they get the ball in the hole sooner than the members of your control group do. Damisch would say that when you activated their superstitions, you increased their self-efficacy and that's what really caused them to do better than your control group.

## WHY IT MATTERS

This study should activate your critical thinking. Luck is a fuzzy idea that we bend to our use when we're faced with things we don't have much control over. This study shows that when luck "works" it has more to do with our own sense of confidence that we'll succeed. But I'll probably still knock on wood occasionally.

# WHERE DISCRIMINATION BEGINS

## *THOSE PEOPLE ARE ALL THE SAME!*

**PSYCH CONCEPT:** Prejudice and Discrimination

**NAME OF EXPERIMENT:** Experimental Study of Positive and Negative Intergroup Attitudes Between Experimentally Produced Groups: Robbers Cave Study

**ORIGINAL SCIENTIST/RESEARCH:** Muzafer Sherif (1954)

**NAME OF REPLICATION/EXTENSION:** Experiments in Intergroup Discrimination

**REPLICATION SCIENTIST/RESEARCH:** Henri Tajfel (1970)

SOCIAL

You may not have given this much thought, but in addition to your sense of who you are as a person (your personal identity) you probably include what psychologists call social identities. These are the groups you belong to. For example, you may be a big fan of a particular sports team. You may strongly identify with the school you go to (or went to), a club you belong to, or a musical group you really like.

Okay, you say, but why is this of much importance? Believe it or not, these social identities are the beginnings of discrimination and prejudice. Part of feeling good about ourselves is our desire to feel good about the groups we belong to. When your sports team wins a game you feel good. When they lose you feel bad. If you find out that someone in your school went to jail or did something else wrong, you feel bad—even if you don't even know that person well. If it hurts the group you belong to, it feels bad to you.

Because we like to see our groups in a positive light, we tend to see other groups in a very singular and often negative way. That's where expressions like "those people" come from. While we may delight in how quirky and fun our own group's members are, we stereotype out-group members: they're all the same and we don't like them.

Muzafer Sherif conducted one of the most famous studies in psychology on this topic. We can take one of the follow-up studies, conducted by Henri Tajfel, and replicate it ourselves in what I think you'll find to be a very interesting experiment.

## THE ORIGINAL EXPERIMENT

Sherif conducted what has become known as the "Robbers Cave" study because it took place in a state park of the same name located in the state of Oklahoma. In 1954, as part of a field experiment, he brought a group of twelve-year-old boys to the park for the purpose of studying inter-group conflict. He split the boys into two groups and asked them to create names for their groups (they did—the "Eagles" and the "Rattlers"). He discovered that he didn't need to do much beyond creating a few competitive activities to quickly create conflict between the groups. They started calling each other names, stealing from each other, and getting into fights. A sense of in-group/out-group feelings had begun.

Now you might think there's no way you could replicate a field experiment like this. You don't have to. As psychologist Henri Tajfel discovered, you don't have to do very much at all to create conflict among groups. We'll replicate Tajfel's unique and fun approach.

## LET'S TRY IT!

Tajfel created groups using a "minimal group" assignment process. He had his participants guessing the number of dots on a page and then playing a game to see if competition developed among them on its own.

Here's what you'll need:

- 2 groups of participants of about 10 people each. The first group should arrive at your selected location (your "lab") at one time and the other group of 10 at a different time (at least 2 hours apart or on different days)
- Black felt marker
- Big room (classroom size would be best, or you could use a garage)
- Large spiral notepad, 8½" × 11" would do
- Coin
- A memory game similar in style to Concentration that you could display in front of the group

It would be ideal if you could project your game from a computer to the front of the class or a projection screen so that everyone in the large room can watch as the game is played. A lot of different video games can work, but you don't want a game that necessarily involves competition between groups. You should be able to find a free Concentration-style game online or on your smartphone or tablet.

## WHAT TO DO:

### GROUP A
- **STEP 1:** This will be your "Estimators" group. Before they arrive, make a list from 1 to whatever number of people you're expecting and write each name next to a number. It would be best if you have an even number of people but it's okay if this doesn't happen. Write an $O$ next to the even-numbered people and a $U$ next to the odd-numbered ones. You'll see why in a second.
- **STEP 2:** The other thing you need to do before everyone arrives is to prepare a separate page on your notebook for each person. On each page put a whole bunch of dots—a different number of dots on each page. You're going to be asking people to guess the

number of dots on their particular page, so make enough dots that they can't count them but not so many that you can't make out one dot from another. On the back page write a number in the upper right corner—any number you want. We'll pretend that this number is the actual number of dots on the other side; however, it doesn't matter what this number is or that you don't know the exact number of dots on the page. Again, you'll see why in a second.

- **STEP 3:** Once you've got your materials from steps 1 and 2 ready, have everyone enter the room. Tell them you're doing a study on memory and that you'll be playing a memory game, but that before you let them play the game you're going to put them into groups based on how close they are to guessing the number of dots on a sheet of paper.

- **STEP 4:** Show each person a different page containing a different number of dots. Tell them that a guess below the actual number of dots means they are "Underestimators" and they should stand on the right side of the room. If their guess is higher than the actual number they are "Overestimators" and should stand on the left side of the room. You probably don't know the actual number of dots and there's no need to count them. If they ask what the total is, tell them that you'll let them know once the study is over. At that point it won't matter, but if they want to count the dots at that time I suppose they can.

- **STEP 5:** That's it. Show each person a page with dots and ask them to guess how many total dots they see. After they give you a number, look on the back of the sheet and pretend to look at the actual number of dots. Then tell each person whether he or she is an underestimator or overestimator. Assign them to a group based on whether you put an *O* (overestimator) or a *U* (underestimator) next to their name on the list you created before they came into the room (have that list placed discreetly near you so you can look at it before you assign someone). What you're doing is creating groups based on the most ridiculous of reasons.

- **STEP 6:** Once you have half your group on one side of the room and half on the other, let one group play the Concentration-style game you chose. When they guess all the tiles, let the other group play. Don't tell them it's a competition.
- **STEP 7:** Play as many "rounds" of the game as you like. Observe their behavior carefully, particularly what members of each group say about members of the other group.
- **STEP 8:** When the games are done, debrief your participants by telling them what you were really looking at.

### GROUP B

- **STEP 1:** This will be your comparison group. You're not going to separate these participants into groups. Have your Concentration-style game up and ready on a screen in the front of the room so everybody can see what's happening on the screen.
- **STEP 2:** Invite everyone to enter the room. Tell them that you're doing a study on memory and that you want them to play your Concentration game. Play your game a few times and notice what happens among the group members. Actually, nothing much interesting should happen. They'll all play your game and it'll be over in about a half hour at most.

## THE RESULTS

So what were you really looking at? In group B you didn't make any group assignments, so everyone should work together, support and encourage each other, and you shouldn't notice any signs of playful name calling, or pointing and laughing. In your "Estimators" groups, however, you'll be surprised that each group not only cheers for its own group members, but "underestimators" will make fun of the performance of "overestimators" and vice versa. All this is based on the most silly of reasons to be in a group: whether they were under or over in their estimations of dots.

It's understandable when prejudice and discrimination forms when there are very clear differences between people and when resources are scarce (this is called the "realistic conflict" theory). As the movie and play *West Side Story* so clearly points out, people of different nationalities and who live in different parts of town can conflict. But what this replication shows is how frighteningly easy it is to create groups that quickly start making fun of each other. One way to break down prejudice and discrimination is to get the two conflicting groups to work together toward the same goal. When group members see that "we're all in this together," the walls between groups break down.

# YOU'RE REALLY NOT GIVING THIS MUCH THOUGHT

## YOU'RE BEING FRAMED!

**PSYCH CONCEPT:** Decision Making

**NAME OF EXPERIMENT:** Rational Choice and the Framing of Decisions

**ORIGINAL SCIENTIST/RESEARCH:** Amos Tversky and Daniel Kahneman (1986)

COGNITION

Advertisers, politicians, and salespeople in all kinds of businesses are trying to persuade you every day. They want to get you to think the way they want you to think so that you'll buy their product or vote for them in the next election. For example, imagine this: you're in a super-market and you're trying to decide which package of steak to buy. Would you buy the one with the little sticker that says "25 Percent Fat" (hmm . . . doesn't sound so good) or the package with the sticker that says "75 Percent Lean" (sounds much healthier).

The way information is presented to you—how it is worded—is what psychologists call "framing." How is the situation framed when someone tells you about it? For example, are we experiencing "global warming"? You may not think so if it's a particularly cold day in January. People tend to rely on their immediate experience. But what about the idea of "climate change"? That way of framing the issue is less likely to get you thinking about whether you are currently feeling hot or cold.

So advertisers use framing, and so do politicians. Let's see how framing could have life-or-death consequences.

# THE ORIGINAL EXPERIMENT

Two well-known psychologists, Daniel Kahneman and Amos Tversky, gave us a lot of insight into how we think. They made us realize that we are not as rational as we would like to think we are.

They presented participants with this hypothetical problem:

Imagine that the U.S. is preparing for the outbreak of an unusual disease, which is expected to kill 600 people. Two alternative programs to combat the disease have been proposed. Which program do you think most people chose:

1. If Program A is adopted, 200 people will be saved.
2. If Program B is adopted, there is $\frac{1}{3}$ probability that 600 people will be saved, and $\frac{2}{3}$ probability that no people will be saved.

Most people went with program A. It just sounds better (more people saved) and less complicated. Of course, the number of people saved is the same for both programs.

Very often we just don't really think through complicated decisions. We go with gut reactions, and we are influenced by what our attention is drawn to.

## LET'S TRY IT!

You can replicate this study in the same way it was originally carried out. You could tell your participants that you are doing a study on decision making, but that might make them give this problem greater attention than if you tell them that you're just "interested in what people think." Just make sure to debrief your participants after they have made their decision by telling them that most of us are "risk averse" and we go with the program that is framed in the most straightforward way and which appears to save the most lives.

Here's what you'll need:

- Group of participants
- Paper with question and options printed on it
- Writing implements

## WHAT TO DO:

- **STEP 1:** Give each person a piece of paper with the following printed on it and ask them to circle the program they prefer:

Imagine that the U.S. is preparing for the outbreak of an unusual disease, which is expected to kill 600 people. Two alternative programs to combat the disease have been proposed. Which program do you think most people chose:

If Program A is adopted, 200 people will be saved.
If Program B is adopted, there is ⅓ probability that 600 people will be saved, and ⅔ probability that no people will be saved.

- **STEP 2:** Tell your participants to circle their preferred option.
- **STEP 3:** Tell your participants what the study is about.
- **STEP 4:** If you're particularly ambitious, you could try this same problem with another group of participants but give them these options:

If Program A is adopted, 400 people will die.
If Program B is adopted, there is ⅓ probability that nobody will die, and ⅔ probability that 600 people will die.

- **STEP 5:** Tell you participants to circle their answer.

## THE RESULTS

Nobody wants anyone to die, and even though the same number of people will die in either of these programs, you'll probably find that most people (Kahneman and Tversky found the numbers to be around 78 percent) prefer the option in which it appears that either a lot of people (200) will be saved or a lot of people will not die (400).

## WHY IT MATTERS

Hopefully, you'll never be involved in a life-or-death decision like the one used for this study, but this framing effect is always being used on you. Have you ever heard someone on TV, who's trying to get you to spend your money, claim that the cost of the product is "only pennies a day!"? That's a framing effect at work. How about this one: "For the cost of a cup of coffee a day . . ."? Again, this is framing. It's used all the time, whether to get you to buy a product or give money to charity. The only way to know if it's a good decision is to think carefully about it. And advertisers are hoping that this is exactly what you will not do.

# THE DEVELOPMENT OF MORAL THINKING

## THAT'S JUST NOT RIGHT!

**PSYCH CONCEPT:** Morality

**NAME OF EXPERIMENT:** The Development of Modes of Thinking and Choices in Years 10 to 16

**ORIGINAL SCIENTIST/RESEARCH:** Lawrence Kohlberg (1958)

**NAME OF REPLICATION/EXTENSION:** In a Different Voice: Women's Conceptions of Self and of Morality

**REPLICATION SCIENTIST/RESEARCH:** Carol Gilligan (1997)

COGNITION

When it comes to really difficult decisions, how do we know what the right thing is to do? As it turns out, whether we think a decision is right or wrong depends on our age and upon whether we think about what other people would do in our situation, or whether we go further and develop our own set of internal standards about right and wrong. Let's take a look at how psychologists study how we make decisions about right and wrong.

## THE ORIGINAL EXPERIMENT

Kohlberg's work is not an "experiment" in the classic sense (where you have group A and group B), but rather a series of carefully controlled studies of children of various ages. Kohlberg presented children, adolescents, and adults with stories that presented an ethical dilemma in which a person was faced with making a very difficult decision. Kohlberg was not interested in the exact decision the child suggested for the person; he was interested in the reasons each person gave for the decision. The most famous story is the one involving the dilemma facing "Heinz":

A woman was near death from a special kind of cancer. There was one drug that the doctors thought might save her. It was a form of radium that a druggist in the same town had recently discovered. The drug was expensive to make, but the druggist was charging ten times what the drug cost him to produce. He paid $200 for the radium and charged $2,000 for a small dose of the drug. The sick woman's husband, Heinz, went to everyone he knew to borrow the money, but he could only get together about $1,000, which is half of what it cost. He told the druggist that his wife was dying and asked him to sell it cheaper or let him pay later. But the druggist said: "No, I discovered the drug and I'm going to make money from it." So Heinz got desperate and broke into the man's laboratory to steal the drug for his wife. Should Heinz have broken into the laboratory to steal the drug for his wife? Why or why not?

As you can imagine, older people gave more complex answers than younger ones. Kohlberg categorized the answers into three levels, each of which contained two stages. We'll focus on the three main levels. Since most people explain their behavior by referring to what others would do, he decided to use the word "conventional" for that level. He referred to thinking less advanced than this as "pre-conventional" and thinking that was more advanced than this as "post-conventional."

1. **Will I get in trouble? (Pre-conventional level):** When it comes to matters like stealing, what are children most worried about? Getting in trouble. That's the focus of the reasoning of people whose answers fell into this category: whether they think Heinz should steal the drug or not, they're concerned about how authority figures will react. So they might say yes—Heinz should steal the drug because otherwise his wife will die and he'll be arrested.

The Development of Moral Thinking

Or they might say no—Heinz should not steal the drug because he'll get arrested. Children age ten and under typically gave these kinds of answers.

2. **What would other people do? (Conventional level):** Adolescents, not surprisingly, are often focused on what others think of them, and this is true of their moral decisions as well. So whether they said yes or no to the drug stealing problem, the reasons had to do with what other people would think of the decision they made, or what they know about society's expectations regarding problems like this. Their "world" is larger than the child's world.

3. **What is the right thing to do? (Post-conventional level):** Typically adults think at this level, though Kohlberg found that not all adults reach this stage. There is no concern with getting in trouble or with what others think or even with society's rules. The person is able to give a complex answer that reflects what they think is the right thing to do.

## LET'S TRY IT!

Here's what you'll need to conduct this experiment yourself:

- Participants under 10 years of age
- Adolescent participants
- Adult participants
- Paper with "Heinz" story printed on it (or another moral dilemma of your choice)
- Writing implements

### WHAT TO DO:
- **STEP 1:** You'll want to work with one participant at a time. Give your participant the story to read (you may have to read the story to the younger children).

- **STEP 2:** Have your participant write down his or her answer to the moral dilemma (for younger children, you can record what they tell you).
- **STEP 3:** If you want to update this study, you can do that by using a difficult moral issue facing society today. For example, several years ago it was discovered that the CIA in the United States was using torture to try to get information regarding terrorism from prisoners. You could ask adolescents and adults their opinion on this. Were the methods they used (for example, "waterboarding") justified?

## THE RESULTS

You'll probably find that whether people think Heinz should or should not steal the drug, children under the age of ten do indeed base that decision on what authority figures in their lives would think or do to them. Adolescents, on the other hand, will refer to what others would do or think (or refer to society's rules regarding this behavior). Many adults will give answers similar to those of adolescents. Some, however, will tell you their personal philosophy regarding when it is right and wrong to steal. If they do, you'll know you're dealing with someone at the "top" of Kohlberg's levels.

Regarding the torture decision: was it okay to do because some other countries also do it (conventional)? Was it not okay because most other countries don't do it (still conventional)? Was it okay because no matter what other people think, we needed that information to save lives (post-conventional)? Or is torture simply never justified (also post-conventional)?

Psychologist Carol Gilligan noticed that Kohlberg used males as his subjects in all of his work. Gilligan studied moral thinking, and she included females in her samples. She found that in addition to the reasons Kohlberg found, women often also considered what effect Heinz's decision would have on the people in his life. What responsibility did he have to care for others? Similarly, another factor you could consider in the torture dilemma is what our responsibility is to the prisoners under our care. What about their pain and suffering? This needs to be considered in our decisions regarding how to act.

You'll see this conflict between moral strategies in the movies. Look for instances where there's a difficult decision to be made. You'll find that the male characters will probably use conventional levels of reasoning, which puts them in conflict (the source of all drama) with the females characters who will emphasize the potential pain and suffering of others.

## WHY IT MATTERS

At some point or another you'll be asked to make a difficult decision. Perhaps this will occur when you are called upon to serve on a jury. The truth about what happened will be hard to determine because different people saw or believe different things, and we know that lawyers will emphasize the things they want you to consider most important. At some point it'll be left up to you to decide. Make sure that you don't make a snap decision. You need to figure out whether what the person did is right or wrong according to society's laws (conventional level) but also consider whether what the person did is right or wrong on a "universal" level (post-conventional). Finally, consider what effect your decision will have on the other people in the person's life. What responsibility do we have to those affected by the decision?

# HOW CHILDREN THINK DIFFERENTLY AS THEY GROW

## THIS ONE HAS MORE! NO, THAT ONE HAS MORE!

**PSYCH CONCEPT:** Cognitive Development, Conservation of Energy

**NAME OF EXPERIMENT:** The Origins of Intelligence in Children

**ORIGINAL SCIENTIST/RESEARCH:** Jean Piaget (1952)

**NAME OF REPLICATION/EXTENSION:** The Potency of Context in Children's Cognition: An Illustration Through Conservation

**REPLICATION SCIENTIST/RESEARCH:** Susan A. Rose and Marion Blank (1974)

COGNITION

Jean Piaget was hugely influential in our understanding of how children's thinking changes as they grow. He developed four stages of cognitive development:

1. **Sensorimotor (0–2 years of age):** If you've ever babysat or observed children of this age, you know that their world is defined by what they can touch and put in their mouths. This is the period of time during which children learn that objects that are not in their sight actually continue to exist (object permanence).

2. **Preoperational (approximately 3–6 years of age):** Children at this stage have not developed the ability to think logically. There is a lot of "magical thinking" at this period of life. Children do a lot of pretending at this age, and it seems to them that just about anything is possible. We'll see an example of this in the study that you can re-create.

3. **Concrete Operations (approximately 7–11 years of age):** At this point, youngsters can understand basic logic problems. Although

abstract thinking isn't yet possible, youngsters can handle some pretty complex concrete math problems.

4. **Formal Operations (approximately 12–late teens):** At this age more complex thought is possible, such as the ability to solve math problems that use symbols instead of just numbers.

Let's take a look at one concept that's a little controversial. Piaget didn't think children in his second stage were capable of logical thought. Rose and Blank said yes they are, and that Piaget didn't conduct his experiment quite right. Let's see who's right.

## THE ORIGINAL EXPERIMENT

Among the many tasks that Piaget gave children at different ages are what he referred to as "conservation" tasks. In the most well-known task (you can find plenty of videos about this on YouTube) he showed children two glasses of the same size that were both half-full of water. The children recognized that they both contained the same amount of water. Then he poured the water from one glass into a taller, thinner glass. The water level appeared to be higher, and despite the fact that the children saw the water being poured into the glass, they said that this taller glass contained more water than the shorter one.

Piaget created quite a number of these small tasks to see what children understood and what they did not yet understand about the world around them. You can easily re-create these little studies.

## LET'S TRY IT!

Here's what you'll need:

- 10 (4- to 5-year-old) children (maybe you can get their parents' permission from a local child care facility)
- Small table

- 10 coins
- 2 glasses of the exact same size
- 1 tall, skinny glass
- Pitcher of water

## WHAT TO DO:

### GROUP A

- **STEP 1:** Take half of the number of children you have available to use in your study. Sit this group in front of you at a table. Put two rows of coins in front of them. Both rows should have five coins, and the second row of coins should be lined up exactly below the first row.
- **STEP 2:** Ask the children if the two rows contain the same number of coins. They may count the coins and will probably say that they're the same.
- **STEP 3:** Next spread out the coins in the top row so that they are a little farther apart than in the bottom row. Again ask if the two rows contain the same number of coins.
- **STEP 4:** Get out the two glasses for your second task. Sit the children in front of you at a table as before. Pour out exactly the same amount of water into each glass.
- **STEP 5:** Ask the children if the two glasses contain the same amount of water. You'll probably get a yes.
- **STEP 6:** Then pour one glass of water into the tall, skinny glass. Ask the children the question again.
- **STEP 7:** Record the children's answers.

### GROUP B

- **STEP 1:** For the second half of your group, you're going to do almost the same thing except that you're not going to ask two questions. Before the children come into the room, have ready on the table the two rows of coins in which one is spread out more than the other, and the water already poured into glasses of different heights.

- **STEP 2:** Ask the children one question for each condition: 1) Do the two rows of coins contain the same number of coins, or does one have more? and 2) Do the two glasses contain the same amount of water, or does one have more?
- **STEP 3:** Record the children's answers.

## THE RESULTS

The children in group A will probably give you the same answers that Piaget got: after the second question they will think that the wider row of coins contains more coins and that the taller glass contains more water. The children are focusing on the most obvious features of the coins and glasses and don't yet understand more complex realities, like volume and size and how those properties don't change just because the outward appearance of an object has changed.

Many (but maybe not all) of the children in group B will get the question right: that the two glasses contain the same amount of water and that the two rows contain the same number of coins.

What Rose and Blank showed us is that Piaget didn't realize that there are social factors as well as cognitive ones at play in his research. Children want to please adults. When you ask a child the same question twice, as you did for the children in group A, there's a good chance they will think that since you're asking the same question twice, their first answer must have been wrong and they should change it.

## WHY IT MATTERS

If we're going to help children learn we need to know what they're capable of at each stage of life. Piaget's guidelines about what a child is capable of doing at different stages is very helpful. What Rose and Blank showed us is that we need to take the context into account, that is, how we ask our questions and in what order we ask them when we're trying to really nail down what children can and cannot do. This is what's so great about the scientific process: as confident as Piaget was, we don't say that he proved anything. His findings lent support to his theory of how children change as they grow, and Rose and Blank's study adds a bit of important subtlety. When we consider these studies together we understand children much better, and this will help us to help them learn as they grow.

# PERSUADING PEOPLE BY FIRST ASKING FOR THE IMPOSSIBLE

## HECK, NO WAY!

**PSYCH CONCEPT:** Door in the Face, Persuasion

**NAME OF EXPERIMENT:** Reciprocal Concessions Procedure for Inducing Compliance: The Door-in-the-Face Technique

**ORIGINAL SCIENTIST/RESEARCH:** Robert B. Cialdini, Joyce E. Vincent, Stephen K. Lewis, Jose Catalan, Diane Wheeler, and Betty Lee Darby (1975)

**NAME OF REPLICATION/EXTENSION:** Is It a Game? Evidence for Social Influence in the Virtual World

**REPLICATION SCIENTIST/RESEARCH:** Paul W. Eastwick and Wendi L. Gardner (2009)

SOCIAL

Have you ever asked your parents for a little money and then when they said okay, you ask them for a little more money than the amount you originally asked for? Psychologists call that the "foot-in-the-door" technique. That is, once you're granted a request for a small favor it becomes more likely that people will give you something a little larger.

However, there's another way to do this: ask your parents for a lot of money up front. After they say, "No way—you've got to be kidding!" then ask for a smaller amount (which is actually the amount you were hoping to get originally). This second approach is what's called the "door-in-the-face" technique. All of us use these tactics at one time or another.

Psychologist Robert Cialdini has done the most to uncover many different persuasion tactics used by children and salespeople alike. Let's see if we can replicate one of his original studies on the door-in-the-face technique.

## THE ORIGINAL EXPERIMENT

Cialdini first decided on a favor he would request of people (college students in this case) that he knew they would absolutely not agree to (what he called an "extreme request"). Here's what he came up with:

> We're currently recruiting university students to work as voluntary, nonpaid counselors at the County Juvenile Detention Center. The position could require two hours of your time per week for a minimum of two years. You would be working more in the line of a Big Brother (Sister) to one of the boys (girls) at the detention home. Would you be interested in being considered for one of these positions?

Would you agree to give up two years of your life like this? I'm betting the answer is no. Cialdini's researchers asked fifty-eight students this question and only two hardy souls said they would do it (3 percent).

Then Cialdini came up with a request that was more moderate—two hours of your time to take some kids to the zoo:

> We're recruiting university students to chaperone a group of boys (girls) from the County Juvenile Detention Center on a trip to the zoo. It would be voluntary, nonpaid, and would require about two hours of one afternoon or evening. Would you be interested in being considered for one of these positions?

He found that about 33 percent of the people he asked agreed to do this favor.

Here's the tricky part: sometimes he first asked someone the extreme request and got the expected No answer. Then he immediately followed up with the moderate request. When the moderate request was asked in this way, over half of these people (55 percent) agreed to do the moderate request.

Now we'll see if we can do the old "door-in-the-face" technique. Let's see how Eastwick and Gardner did this study in a virtual world.

## LET'S TRY IT!

You can do this study with people you know in a face-to-face fashion, but Eastwick and Gardner decided to see if this door-in-the-face method worked in a virtual world. Here's what you'll need to replicate this study:

- Access to a computer with a virtual world account

### WHAT TO DO:
- **STEP 1:** If you don't already have one, get an account or log in to your account in a virtual world. Eastwick and Gardner chose to use There.com, but you could use Secondlife.com or some other online virtual world you're familiar with.

### GROUP A: MODERATE REQUEST
Eastwick and Gardner tried to find out how many people would agree to this moderate request: "Hi, I'm doing a photo scavenger hunt. Would you teleport to Duda Beach with me and let me take a screenshot of you?"

"Duda Beach" was a location inside There.com, so you could use this location or chose another one from the virtual world you're located in.

- **STEP 1:** Go into your virtual world and approach someone who is standing alone or who is among others but not currently engaged in conversation.
- **STEP 2:** Once someone says "hi" back, ask them your moderate question about teleporting to another location for a screenshot. Ask twenty avatars and count the number who say yes.

- **STEP 3:** When they say yes, follow through with your request and teleport with them. They won't know if you've taken a screenshot, but you can do that and then later label it as someone in group A.
- **STEP 4:** Thank them for this assistance.

## GROUP B: FOOT-IN-THE-DOOR REQUEST
This time we'll use the foot-in-the-door technique and see if we can get more people to teleport with us.

- **STEP 1:** Approach someone who's not busy and ask them if you can do something really, really simple. Eastwick asked this question: "Can I take a screenshot of you?" Probably everyone will say yes.
- **STEP 2:** Next you ask the moderate question: "Thanks. Now, would you teleport to _____ with me and let me take a screenshot of you?" Fill in the blank with whatever location you decided to use.
- **STEP 3:** Teleport if they say yes and record which group the person was in.

## GROUP C: DOOR-IN-THE-FACE REQUEST
Now we'll use the door-in-the-face technique.

- **STEP 1:** As before, find someone who isn't busy but first ask a question that is similar to what Eastwick asked: "I need to take a screenshot of someone in 50 different locations. It's supposed to take about 2 hours of teleporting and traveling. Would you do it?"
- **STEP 2:** I guarantee nobody will say yes to that. Then follow up with a moderate question: "Okay, I understand. Well then would you teleport to _____ with me and let me take a screenshot of you?"
- **STEP 3:** If they say yes, do the teleporting and record what happened.

## THE RESULTS

I think you'll find that the number of avatars that say yes to your moderate question will be far higher in conditions B and C. The explanation for why we do agree to a request once the foot-in-the-door technique has been used on us is that after agreeing to a request, we tend to see ourselves as helpful people so we agree again. As for the door-in-the-face technique: the theory is that once we say no we feel a little bad about it and then the other person asks for something that now, in comparison, seems pretty trivial, so we go along with it.

## WHY IT MATTERS

These are powerful persuasion tactics. You can use them when you're trying to persuade people or, since you now know about them, you'll be more aware of when they're being used on you and can resist the temptation to go along with the tactic. These tactics are used by salespeople of all kinds, so beware!

# THE PSYCHOLOGY OF HUMOR

## THAT'S NOT FUNNY!

**PSYCH CONCEPT:** Humor
**NAME OF EXPERIMENT:** Quirkology
**ORIGINAL SCIENTIST/RESEARCH:** Richard Wiseman (2007)

COGNITION

Psychologists study all kinds of things about people that you probably think can't be studied scientifically. How, you ask, can the feeling of love possibly be studied in a laboratory? You'd be surprised. Just check out the *Psychology of Attractiveness Podcast* to find out. But in this experiment we're going to look at humor. Why are some jokes funny to you and some fall flat?

Have you ever told a joke that you think is hilarious but nobody laughed? Or they gave you one of those "polite laughs" and you know they really didn't find it funny? Is there one joke that's a sure thing? A joke that everyone will laugh at? Turns out there is—well, 95 percent of people will laugh at it anyway. You'll learn what that joke is in the next section, and will also find out why some jokes are funnier than others to you. We can even do a little experimenting with jokes. Let's get started.

## THE ORIGINAL EXPERIMENT

Psychologist Richard Wiseman got a great idea back in 2001: why don't we set up a website where people can easily submit what they think is the funniest joke they ever heard and let everybody vote until we've got the funniest joke in the world? This will also give us a huge database of jokes that will help us learn why some jokes "work" almost all the time while others don't.

After receiving over 40,000 jokes, the winner—the joke rated by Wiseman and his colleagues most highly on their 1–5 scale (which they call their "Giggleometer")—is this one:

> A couple of New Jersey hunters are out in the woods when one of them falls to the ground. He doesn't seem to be breathing, his eyes are rolled back in his head. The other guy whips out his cell phone and calls the emergency services. He gasps to the operator: "My friend is dead! What can I do?" The operator, in a calm soothing voice says: "Just take it easy. I can help. First, let's make sure he's dead." There is a silence, then a shot is heard. The guy's voice comes back on the line. He says: "Okay, now what?"

I'm going to guess that you at least have a little smile on your face. So why is it funny? Wiseman says that the joke is an example of a key ingredient of all funny jokes: they allow us to feel superior to others. Not the most admirable thing about human beings, but let's admit it: it is indeed funnier when someone else falls down than when we fall down. The joke makes us feel a tiny bit better about ourselves.

Let's put one of Wiseman's "Laughlab" jokes to the test.

## LET'S TRY IT!

Here's another joke. How highly do you think people would rate it on Wiseman's 1–5 Giggleometer?

> A man in his late sixties suspects that his wife is going deaf, so he decides to test her hearing. He stands on the opposite side of the living room from her and asks: "Can you hear me?" No answer. He moves halfway across the room toward her and asks, "Can you hear me now?"

No answer. He moves and stands right beside her and says: "Can you hear me now?" She replies: "For the third time, yes!"

Older people think this is funny. Younger people don't. Why? Because, Wiseman says, it addresses something that older people are anxious about: their hearing. Young people understand the joke and will probably give you one of those polite smiles and a nod, but they won't think it's that funny because they aren't worried about their hearing. So in addition to superiority, anxiety is another factor that explains why we think some jokes are funny and others aren't.

Here's another joke that Wiseman found. Younger people (especially women) think this one is funny:

A husband stepped on one of those penny scales that tell you your fortune and weight and dropped in a coin. "Listen to this," he said to his wife, showing her a small white card. "It says I'm energetic, bright, resourceful, and a great person." "Yeah," his wife nodded, "and it has your weight wrong, too."

So here's what you could do to see if Wiseman's findings about jokes—and especially about the role of anxiety—is on the mark. Here's what you'll need:

- Group of younger participants (say, in their 20s and 30s)
- Group of older participants (above 60)
- Previous two jokes

**WHAT TO DO:**
- **STEP 1:** First memorize the two jokes in the preceding sections.
- **STEP 2:** Tell the jokes to your group of younger people and your group of older people.

- **STEP 3:** Each time you tell one of the jokes ask each person to rate the joke on a 1–10 scale. (We're using a larger scale than Wiseman's just to see if we're more likely to catch subtle differences in taste.)

## THE RESULTS

As odd as it sounds, I think you'll find that Wiseman has identified an important component of humor—anxiety. You'll get a higher number on your 1–10 "funny scale" from older people for the "deaf old man" joke than you will for the "husband" joke, and you'll get higher scores from younger people for the "husband" joke.

## WHY IT MATTERS

Understanding why some things are funny may be most important to comedians (though I'm going to guess that they trust their gut more than the scientific literature). But I'll bet comedians know about superiority and anxiety at a "gut" level. And this comes back to advice you've probably heard about how to give an effective speech: know your audience.

# A BETTER WAY TO DETECT LIES

*YOU LIAR!*

**PSYCH CONCEPT:** Lie Detecting
**NAME OF EXPERIMENT:** Drawings As an Innovative and Successful Lie Detection Tool
**ORIGINAL SCIENTIST/RESEARCH:** Aldert Vrij, Sharon Leal, Samantha Mann, Lara Warmelink, Par Anders Granhag, and Ronald P. Fisher (2009)

COGNITION

You're a secret agent on a mission. Should you decide to accept it, your mission is to pick up the "package" from Agent A and deliver it to another location. Oh by the way, you might be intercepted along the way, and if they're the "bad guys" make sure to lie about where you picked up the package.

Some researchers really know how to have fun. Vrij and colleagues did just that when they looked at what is perhaps a new way to detect when someone is lying: ask them to draw a picture of where they were at the time of the crime.

You see, no matter what you may see in the movies, we really don't have a good lie detecting system and there is no so-called "truth serum." There are drugs that will make you drowsy and more likely to talk, but what you say isn't any more likely to be the truth than it is to be things you dream up in this altered state.

Vrij and colleagues found an interesting new way to find out if you're lying—a way that involves agents, packages, and bad guys. Let's see how they did it.

You arrive at the "lab" for what will turn out to be the most unusual psychology experiment you'll ever be involved in:

You learn that you will be sent on a mission to receive a package from Agent A at a particular location and to deliver it somewhere else. During the mission you may be intercepted by agents belonging to the organization you are to represent or to a hostile organization. You should reveal the actual details about your mission to friendly agents but make something up about all aspects of your mission to hostile agents.

But how do you know who's friend and who's foe? A secret password of course. After you deliver the package you'll be asked by another agent to come inside to answer some questions. You're to ask this question:

"Do you have the time please?"

If the agent says:

"No sorry, my watch stopped at 6:38 this morning"

Then you'll know the agent is friendly. He'll ask you questions about the mission and you can answer him truthfully. If the agent responds in any way other than the preceding phrase, you're instructed to lie about where you were when you picked up the package.

You are asked several questions about your mission, including one question in which you are asked to draw a picture of where you were when you picked up the package. Those told to lie chose a place along the route, but did not give away the exact location of the drop-off.

Another group of people working with Vrij then read the answers everyone gave to these questions and looked at the drawings. They were not told who was lying and who wasn't. Guess what? They correctly identified the liars 87 percent of the time. How'd they do that? Let's find out as we try this ourselves.

## LET'S TRY IT!

Here's what you'll need:

- 4 friends (fellow researchers): 2 helpers to get your participants to go from start to finish and 2 people to look at their drawings and rate them to see if they can figure out who was lying and who was telling the truth.
- 10–20 participants
- 5–10-minute route for your agents to take
- Small wrapped package. You can wrap a box in a paper bag if you like (and add a little weight to it) just to heighten the drama. But really, it doesn't matter what's in the package.
- Blank pieces of paper and pencils

### WHAT TO DO:
- **STEP 1:** Plan out a route from the starting place of your study to another location (another room on campus, or a room or garage in someone's house). Include some turns. It could be a walking or driving route. Write down your route on pieces of paper to give to your participants.
- **STEP 2:** Pick a point that is halfway through your route where you'll have someone waiting to give your participant/agents the package. This spot could be anything along the way—even a tree.
- **STEP 3:** Instruct your participants to meet you wherever you've determined is the starting place for these "missions." Participants will go through the missions individually.
- **STEP 4:** A participant meets you at the starting point. You tell her she is an agent and you want her to follow the route on the paper. There's a place to stop halfway and meet up with someone who will

give her a package. Tell her she should take the package and continue to the end.

- **STEP 5:** Instruct the participant that at the end of the route she should give the package to the person waiting for her. She should ask the person the question: "Do you have the time please?"
- **STEP 6:** If the person gives the answer, "No sorry, my watch stopped at 6:38 this morning," the participant should answer all the questions truthfully. Any other answer (such as the actual time) and participants should lie about any question they are asked.
- **STEP 7:** After participants (the "agents") have answered all the questions they are sent on their way.
- **STEP 8:** The person at the end of the route should sit the participant down and ask her to "draw the location where you picked up the package."
- **STEP 9:** When the participant is done drawing the location, put a T (for truth—that is, the participants was given the "My watch stopped at 6:38" answer) or L (for lie—the actual time was given to the agent, which means they should have lied when asked a question or asked to draw anything) on the back of the drawing. The study with that participant is then over. Follow this procedure for every participant.
- **STEP 10:** When you've gone through this procedure for all the participants, collect all the drawings, number them in the top right corner, and show them to your two raters. These two people should not know whether the "agent" had to lie or tell the truth based on the other agent's answer to the question.
- **STEP 11:** Working on a piece of paper separate from the drawing itself, each rater should work alone and rate each drawing for the amount of detail it contains. Each should circle a number on this scale for each drawing:

Not detailed   **1**  **2**  **3**  **4**  **5**  **6**  **7**  Very detailed

The raters should also indicate on their separate sheet whether the drawing was done from an "over the shoulder" point of view or a "top down" view.

## THE RESULTS

You should find what Vrij found—that the ratings for the drawings done by those people who had to lie are less detailed than of those who told the truth. Also, Vrij found that "truth-tellers" drew pictures from the "over the shoulder" point of view and "liars" tended to draw pictures from an overhead view. People who are telling the truth are drawing from their memory of where they actually were, so they can include lots of detail and are likely to draw the scene from their perspective. Liars have to make up some location and so probably won't include much detail, and they're more likely to draw it as if they are looking down on the location.

## WHY IT MATTERS

Since the devices and drugs we use as "lie detectors" have a very high failure rate, we need new approaches. The one used here by Vrij and colleagues makes a lot of sense. Maybe this will replace—or at least add to—our toolbox for figuring out who's lying and who's telling the truth.

# YOUR BODY AFFECTS YOUR THINKING

## *WOW—THAT'S A HEAVY IDEA*

**PSYCH CONCEPT:** Embodied Cognition
**NAME OF EXPERIMENT:** Weight As an Embodiment of Importance
**ORIGINAL SCIENTIST/RESEARCH:** Nils B. Jostmann, Daniël Lakens, and Thomas W. Schubert (2009)

COGNITION

Enter into a controversy. Scientists discuss and sometimes they argue. Here's something they're arguing about: replicating our research. The methods of science require that once you think you have found something, you should do the study again to make sure. Then other researchers should conduct your study to see if they find the same thing. Replication. The problem is, we don't really do it often enough. There is a worry that some of the studies that have been published just don't get replicated (replication studies don't tend to get published), or if someone does replicate a study and they don't find the same thing as the original study, the study gets placed in the "file drawer" and nobody finds out that that great idea you heard about doesn't really exist.

Enter the idea of "embodied cognition"—the idea that your body can strongly influence your thinking. For example, if you lean forward, are you more likely to think about the future than if you lean back? Some researchers can find it—others can't. I have to admit I'm a little skeptical myself of some of these studies. How can a simple manipulation of your body have a strong effect on your mind?

In this section we'll talk about a study that found support for this body-mind link. Another study supported the findings. Three others found no support. Maybe you'll break the logjam.

In the famous movie *Back to the Future*, a joke was made regarding the expression "heavy." The character Marty (who is from the future) uses this expression as we know it today—an idea that is difficult or complex is referred to as "heavy." The character "Doc," who in this movie exists in 1955, is not familiar with the use of the word "heavy" in this way and wonders, "Why are things so heavy in the future? Is there a problem with the Earth's gravitational pull?"

We frequently use metaphors like "heavy" and "light" ("He's a lightweight") in our everyday speech. But is it possible that when you're filling out a survey on an important topic, your opinion could be swayed by the weight of the clipboard that you're holding?

## THE ORIGINAL EXPERIMENT

Jostmann, Lakens, and Schubert conducted a rather straightforward study. They came up with some questions and asked students to rate how important the issue is. For example, students were asked how important it was that the student body have a voice in the college decision-making process. Student participants were stopped as they walked across campus and asked to hold a clipboard while they filled out the questionnaire. The researchers expected that if you were holding a heavy clipboard (2.29 pounds or 1,039 grams) you would think the issue is more important (on a 1–7 scale) than if you were holding a light clipboard (1.45 pounds). And that's what they found—an average of 5.27 on the heavy clipboard versus a 4.21 on the light clipboard.

They found similar results with other questions, such as how satisfied they are with the city, the quality of life in the city, and their satisfaction with the mayor.

The idea makes some sense, but four other researchers tried this and couldn't find any effect for the weight of the clipboard. Can you?

## LET'S TRY IT!

Here's all you'll need:

- Light clipboard
- Heavy clipboard
- Plain computer paper (to fill the clipboard compartment)
- Pencil
- 4 questions, each with a 1–7 scale underneath them (1 = not at all important 7 = very important)
- About 30 participants

In regard to the clipboard weight issue Jostmann found a nice solution: use just one clipboard that has a storage compartment. To make it "heavy" they filled the storage compartment with paper. Using the same clipboard is also good so that you're not using a different color clipboard in your "light" and "heavy" conditions.

### WHAT TO DO:

- **STEP 1:** You'll need to come up with your own questions for the survey. You'll have to choose topics that are open-ended and on which there are varying opinions. Remember that it doesn't matter how the person feels about the topic (for or against). We're only looking to see if they think the issue is important.
- **STEP 2:** Try to ask about thirty participants—fifteen answering your questions when the questionnaire is clipped to the clipboard when the compartment is empty, and fifteen answering the questions when the compartment is full.

## THE RESULTS

Because of the controversy surrounding this issue, I don't really know how this is going to go. Jostmann thinks you'll find what he found— but lots of other researchers didn't find a thing.

## WHY IT MATTERS

If Jostmann is right, think about the implications: if you want survey recipients to really take an issue seriously, just put the question on a heavy clipboard! What a simple tactic that could be for politicians and marketers. Or is it a waste of time? The Jostmann finding was surprising and a little fun, so it got some headline coverage and a lot of people now think that this is a real effect. The four replication experiments that didn't find a thing received no press at all. Remember that when a researcher finds something "statistically significant," as Jostmann did, it just means that what he found is an unlikely event but it could still have happened by chance. The only way to have real confidence is to replicate studies over and over again and get similar results each time, which is what this book is all about.

# THE CAUSES OF JOB SATISFACTION

## TAKE THIS JOB AND . . .

**PSYCH CONCEPT:** The Two-Factor Theory of Job Satisfaction and Motivation

**NAME OF EXPERIMENT:** One More Time: How Do You Motivate Employees?

**ORIGINAL SCIENTIST/RESEARCH:** Frederick Herzberg (1957)

**NAME OF REPLICATION/EXTENSION:** Job Attitudes: Review of Research and Opinion

**REPLICATION SCIENTIST/RESEARCH:** J. Richard Hackman and Greg R. Oldham (1974)

EMOTIONS

Among the many kinds of psychologists are those who are called industrial/organizational psychologists, and no—they don't do therapy in the workplace. In fact, they aren't trained in psychotherapy at all. They are trained to do things like helping managers figure out how to lead and motivate their employees, how to help employees be more productive, and how to select the best people from the many people who apply for a job.

If you look through job descriptions, I'll bet that you'll find the words "highly motivated" among the desired qualities. Motivating employees—or finding out why they aren't motivated—is a tough job. A lot of employees start out motivated and then lose that quality over time. Why? What is it about the workplace that causes some people to work really hard and others not? Herzberg wanted to find out.

## THE ORIGINAL EXPERIMENT

Herzberg's approach was rather straightforward: he asked people what made them feel motivated and happy and what made them feel the opposite way at work. He categorized their answers into what he called "hygiene" and "motivator" factors. Here's an example of each:

### Hygiene Factors
- Your salary
- Your relationship with your boss
- Your relationship with your peers
- The status your job provides you
- Job security

### Motivator Factors
- Getting recognition
- Achieving something
- Have responsibility
- Opportunities to advance
- The work itself is enjoyable

Notice that the hygiene factors are all outside of yourself—they have to do with other people or how the job is set up—while the motivators are more internal, expressing a sense of achievement and growth.

What Herzberg concluded was that jobs that are low in both hygiene and motivator factors result in employees with low motivation and low job satisfaction. But here's a twist: if a job has good job security and a good salary and you have a good relationship with your peers (all hygiene factors) will you be happy? Not really. Herzberg said that while these things are good to have, at most all they'll do is prevent you from being unhappy. Think about it: if your job has good security are you going to jump for joy about it? If your salary is good you'll probably be happy about that for a little while, but after a few years of receiving that salary you'll get used to it (we call this "habituation") and the positive effects will fade away.

The only way to be really happy at your job according to Herzberg is to have one that provides the motivator factors: enjoyable work, recognition, and opportunities for growth.

Not everyone thinks Herzberg's theory is the best. As you probably know, we all have a tendency to blame others when things go wrong and to take credit when things go right (the "self-serving bias"). Herzberg's interviewees may have been doing a lot of this, and it sort of looks like it when you look at these "hygiene" and "motivator" factors.

Let's see what you find.

## LET'S TRY IT!

Replicating Herzberg's study doesn't require much in the way of equipment. Here is all you'll need:

- About 30 participants to interview
- Paper for each interviewee

### WHAT TO DO:
- **STEP 1:** You need to talk with people who have had jobs and ask them what they think made them happy at the job and what made them unhappy.
- **STEP 2:** Be ready with a piece of paper for each interviewee. Put a line down the middle of each sheet and put "Happy" to the left of that line and "Unhappy" to the right. You don't have to record what the participants say or write down every word. In each column just write down words or phrases that they mention when they're talking about being happy or unhappy with their job.

J. Richard Hackman and Greg Oldham also looked into this issue of job satisfaction and motivation. They were aware that Herzberg's approach, while uncovering some good information, had its limitations. Their studies revealed that there were other, subtle factors that were important, such as whether or not the job included much variety from day to day, whether people thought the job was important, whether they could make any decisions about how the work was done, and whether people felt that they experienced a sense of accomplishment from seeing a task from beginning to end. Ask your interviewees if these factors were present (or absent) in your interviews.

## THE RESULTS

When you've talked with about thirty people, take out all your notes and do what we call a "content analysis." Unlike a statistical analysis, a content analysis requires you to read carefully through your notes and look for themes and repeated phrases. You may find what Herzberg found: that jobs people liked were the ones where they felt they were challenged and respected for their input. The factors your interviewees identify for jobs they disliked will probably be matters such as not liking their boss or receiving a low salary.

Look for some of the factors mentioned by Hackman and Oldham: variety, significance, accomplishment, and autonomy. People may not bring these things up at first, but you'll probably find them after a little probing.

## WHY IT MATTERS

Most of us want jobs that we like and that we feel motivated to do. Simply making someone an "employee of the month" is not going to cut it. But what, exactly, should managers do to make jobs more "enriching"? The studies done by both Herzberg and Hackman and Oldham gave us very specific suggestions regarding what can be done. Not all jobs can be made really, really interesting, but all jobs can be redesigned to make them more fun for humans to carry out.

# A PSYCHOLOGICAL BOOSTER SHOT

## *I WOULD NEVER FALL FOR THAT!*

**PSYCH CONCEPT:** Persuasion, Personal Fable, Dopamine, Frontal Lobe
**NAME OF EXPERIMENT:** Dispelling the Illusion of Invulnerability: The Motivations and Mechanisms of Resistance to Persuasion
**ORIGINAL SCIENTIST/RESEARCH:** Brad J. Sagarin, Robert B. Cialdini, William E. Rice, and Sherman B. Serna (2002)

SOCIAL

Teenagers have what psychologists call a "personal fable." That is, they think they are special in some way and that bad things won't happen to them. This is one reason why many teenagers take unnecessary risks. Other reasons include the fact that at this stage of life, when a teenager takes a risk (like perhaps driving too fast) and gets away with it, the reward—in terms of a momentary release of the neurotransmitter dopamine in the brain—is very powerful. Adults forget how powerfully positive (and negative) feelings can be when you're a teen. Also, the frontal lobe of the brain—the part that does all the complex thinking for you—isn't yet fully developed in teens.

The advertising industry is very much aware of these facts and they use them to get teens to buy. Robert Cialdini, who has done the most to make us aware of how we are persuaded every day, identified six tactics used by advertisers:

1. Consistency
2. Liking
3. Authority
4. Scarcity
5. Social Proof
6. Reciprocity

We'll focus here on authority and scarcity, but if you want to learn more about these tactics get Cialdini's book *Influence: Science and Practice*.

This study borrows an idea from the medical field: one way to make sure you don't get a full-blown case of smallpox is to give you a shot containing a small amount of it. Your system can fight this small amount successfully and you'll wind up with an immunity to smallpox.

Can we use this same approach to make you "immune" to the persuasive tactics of advertisers? Let's find out.

## THE ORIGINAL EXPERIMENT

Sagarin and his colleagues know that just telling people about these persuasion tactics and how they work is not going to be enough to lessen their power to influence us. They created a small "experience" for their participants to actually show them how vulnerable they are to the tactics. This experience consisted of showing them an advertisement containing a well-known person (they used Arnold Schwarzenegger) appearing in an advertisement for something he's really not an expert about (Internet-delivered television). Some participants looked at this ad and wrote down their thoughts about it, including how persuasive they thought it was. Turns out it was a pretty persuasive ad. The researchers then showed them how they had been influenced by the presence of an "authority figure" (Schwarzenegger), who, while he might be an authority about some matters (weight lifting), probably isn't an authority on Internet television. How much weight should his opinion count here? Students were convinced of the power of using authority figures in advertising once they reflected on how they had been fooled.

They had been inoculated. And it worked. When they were shown another ad that also used an authority figure, they were more skeptical than participants who hadn't seen the ad with Schwarzenegger. They were also more "persuasion resistant" than participants who were simply informed about how advertisers use well-known people who shouldn't be considered authorities on a product.

Let's see if we can "inoculate" people against the power of persuasive ads.

## LET'S TRY IT!

People are also strongly persuaded when they believe that a product is scarce or that it might not be available for much longer ("This sale ends tomorrow!"). So let's inoculate one group of participants and not inoculate another and then see if any of them fall for false scarcity. Here's what you'll need to prepare:

- 2 groups of participants
- Two products your participants might be interested in buying. See if you can find interesting products they probably don't already own. A few suggestions: pencils shaped like drumsticks (so you can drum the desk while you're thinking), stylish headphones that connect to your cell phone via Bluetooth, or a "desk caddy" for your pencils and pens that is made out of a rare and beautiful wood.
- Advertisement for each of the products
- Writing implements

### WHAT TO DO:
- **STEP 1:** Before you print out any copies of these ads for your participants to look at, find an empty space near the top of the ads and put some text there that hints at the scarcity of the product or the price. For one ad, emphasize the scarcity of the price. Examples of what you can add: "Only available for a short time at this price!" or "Sale ends tomorrow!" For the other ad, emphasize the scarcity of the product itself: "Only 50 of these were made and now only 5 are left!"

- **STEP 2:** At the very bottom of the page, in an empty space, type in this question and the scale:

How persuasive is this ad?

Not at all persuasive   **1 2 3 4 5 6 7 8 9 10**   Very persuasive

- **STEP 3:** Choose one ad (the one emphasizing price scarcity) to be ad A and the other (emphasizing product scarcity) to be ad B. Print out enough copies of ad A to show to all your participants.
- **STEP 4:** Only print out half that many copies of ad B.

### GROUP A: INOCULATION GROUP

- **STEP 1:** Show participants ad B (product scarcity).
- **STEP 2:** Ask them to look at it carefully and then circle an answer on the scale. They'll probably give it a 6 or above.
- **STEP 3:** After they have made their decision, talk to them about the tactic of scarcity and how advertisers use it to try to get you to act. Often this "scarcity" is false: the company can easily make more of the product (especially if it's a digital product like a song or an eBook). This experience of being perhaps a little bit fooled by the ad, along with your discussion about scarcity, is your inoculation process.
- **STEP 4:** Now show participants ad A (price scarcity).
- **STEP 5:** As before, have them look at the ad carefully and circle an answer on the scale.
- **STEP 6:** That's the end of the study for these participants, but of course, feel free to talk to them about the ad and how it also tried to use the scarcity effect (companies can easily extend the amount of time that a price is available).

### GROUP B: CONTROL GROUP

- **STEP 1:** Show this group ad A (price scarcity).
- **STEP 2:** Have them circle a number on the scale.

- **STEP 3:** That's all for this group, but feel free to talk with them about the scarcity tactic as you tell them what you're looking at in this experiment.

## THE RESULTS

Your group B participants will probably give a high rating (7-10) for the product shown in ad A. Your group A participants will probably give the product in ad A a lower rating. That's because they've not only learned how scarcity works, they've also experienced it firsthand and they realize that even they can be influenced by it.

## WHY IT MATTERS

Companies are tying to influence you every day in person and online. You need to be aware of what these influence tactics are and how to not be affected by them. Ask yourself a couple of questions: Is this product truly scarce? Is the authority figure promoting this product truly an expert on products like this? Of course, if you go into advertising or marketing you'll probably be tempted to use these tactics in your work. Let's hope you do so in an ethical way.

# PERCEPTION IS MORE THAN WHAT WE SEE

## *MAKE YOUR OWN ILLUSIONS*

**PSYCH CONCEPT:** Visual Illusions

**NAME OF EXPERIMENT:** Decrement of the Müller-Lyer Illusion with Saccadic and Tracking Eye Movements

**ORIGINAL SCIENTIST/RESEARCH:** Clarke Burnham (1968)

Aside from pictures of cats, visual illusions are an Internet favorite. We like to look at images of things that simply cannot exist, such as those created by M. C. Escher. He created those images of buildings with the impossible stairs that go nowhere or the hands that draw themselves. Search on his name and you'll see plenty of examples.

Psychologists, of course, are interested in these images as well. Why are we tricked? What we've learned over the years is that our minds are very much involved in making sense out of the signals that reach our eyes. But how? How can we see depth when we know an image is flat? Why do lines appear bent when we know they're actually straight? Obviously, we don't see exactly what's in front of our faces. Perhaps the most famous visual illusion is the one created by Franz Müller-Lyer in 1889 (seen to the right).

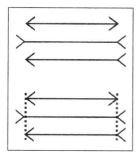

It really is hard to tell that these lines are exactly the same length. Our eyes are drawn outward by the outward-facing "wings" on the line and our eyes are drawn inward by the inward-facing wings. Burnham

and many other researchers have tried to find out how we can lessen the effect of this illusion.

Let's take a look at what they did and then let's create our own visual illusions and see what effect they have on people.

## THE ORIGINAL EXPERIMENT

Burnham wondered whether the Müller-Lyer effect could be lessened (that is, you would see the three lines as close in length) if you looked at the lines differently. We often look at things in our environment using a "saccadic" eye pattern. This means that your eyes are "jumping" from one spot to another. This happens when you're reading, for example, as your eyes jump from one word to another, but also happens when you examine a painting. It is especially observable during the REM (rapid eye movement) stage of sleep when your eyes dart back and forth.

Burnham set up some pretty sophisticated equipment:

> The study was conducted in a lightproof room, and the arrowheads were formed of luminous paint. The two angled lines of each arrowhead were ¼ inch wide and 1¾ inches long and formed an angle of 30 degrees with the horizontal. The standard portion of the illusion, located on the left and consisting of the inward pointing lines, was 6⅞ inches from apex to apex. The apparatus for the Saccadic condition had a light bulb placed at each of the three apexes. The apparatus for the Tracking condition had a single movable bulb attached to a track behind the apparatus. This bulb was moved from apex to apex by a motor and pulley arrangement and was visible throughout its path.

You and I may look at these illusions for fun, but these researchers take their work very seriously. What Burnham found was that the only way to see that the three lines were of equal length was to use eye tracking equipment—tools that keep your eyes very steady while you look up and down the length of the lines. Since we don't ordinarily observe in this way, it's really, really hard to avoid this illusion.

I'm going to bet that you don't have the kind of equipment described by Burnham. That's okay; there are still ways to do a little experimenting with visual illusions. Let's find out how.

## LET'S TRY IT!

The ability to draw amazing illusions like Escher's obviously requires the ability to draw as well as he did. I'm going to assume you don't have that talent. So let's draw the Müller-Lyer illusion using some old-fashioned equipment. What you'll need:

- Pencil
- Protractor
- Blank paper
- The Müller-Lyer illusion

### WHAT TO DO:

You can try this little study on individuals in two groups or put the same people through both A and B below.

### GROUP A

- **STEP 1:** On one piece of paper draw a straight line about 6 inches long. Ask people to draw a dot right in the center of it. This shouldn't be too hard or take too long, and most people should be able to quickly make a spot that is just about at the center.

### GROUP B

- **STEP 1:** Draw another 6-inch line, but this time put "wings" on both sides so it looks like a typical Müller-Lyer image. There are three ways to attach these wings:

1. An arrowhead on both ends of the line
2. An arrowhead on one end and a "tail" on the other
3. Tails on both ends of the line

Create all three types of lines. If you want to be exact about these "wing lines," the angle is 30 degrees between the horizontal line and a wing.

- **STEP 2:** Ask people to draw a dot right in the center of each line.

## THE RESULTS

You'll find that your participants will take a lot longer to find the center of the horizontal line when the Müller-Lyer wings are present. For the line with the arrowhead on one end and a tail at the other, their dot will probably be closer to the end of the line where you drew an arrowhead. The eye is drawn toward the arrowhead and it's hard to resist. For the other two lines, your participants will probably say something like, "Wow—this is hard." And it is. The eye is drawn in different directions and the influence of those "wings" is hard to resist.

## WHY IT MATTERS

These illusions, in addition to being useful for sharing in social networks, remind us that what we ultimately "see" with our eyes is a mix of what's there and what we think should be there. Our brain's sense of what we "should" be seeing is influenced by our past experience with physical objects in the real world and by what we know to be possible and impossible.

# SMARTPHONES: DO THEY HINDER OR IMPROVE OUR LIFE EXPERIENCES?

## HOLD STILL! LET ME TAKE A PICTURE!

**PSYCH CONCEPT:** Engagement/Happiness

**NAME OF EXPERIMENT:** How Taking Photos Increases Enjoyment of Experiences

**ORIGINAL SCIENTIST/RESEARCH:** Kristin Diehl, Gal Zauberman, and Alixandra Barasch (2016)

LEARNING

Some concerts and restaurants actually ban the use of smartphones during the show or dinner. Have you ever had the experience of having your phone taken away because of the belief that taking photos of the event will diminish the experience? Well, researchers have looked into this. A hundred years ago researchers were obsessed with understanding visual illusions. Today we naturally want to find out what effect the ubiquitous cell phone, with its built-in camera, is having on your enjoyment of life.

We have some good ideas as to why your phone is so addictive. Here are a few:

- **Variable rewards:** As B. F. Skinner taught us so long ago, some of the most powerful influencers on our behavior are unexpected rewards. Skinner showed us that the uncertainty of rewards is what can lead to gambling addiction. Same with your cell phone. Every once in a while it dings or makes some other noise and you never know when that signal is going to lead to something rewarding. That's hard to resist.

- **Dopamine and the teenage brain:** Adults get "pings" on their phones too but they don't feel as compelled to check their phone immediately like teens do. Why? Because the tiny release of the neurotransmitter dopamine that occurs just before a reward produces a very powerful effect in teens. Not so for adults. That's why adults can't understand the "pull of the phone."
- **Mystery:** Modern cell phones give us access to a world of information and stimulation. There are questions that need to be answered; puzzles and problems that we find hard to resist. Humans love the unknown.

So what about the camera on your phone? Does using it decrease your enjoyment of what you're currently experiencing? Diehl and her colleagues wanted to find out.

## THE ORIGINAL EXPERIMENT

Some researchers have all the fun. Diehl's study actually contains nine smaller studies. The researchers took participants on bus rides (real and virtual), gave them dinners at a restaurant, and involved them in an arts and crafts project. That last one is the one we're going to do. It'll be fun.

Imagine that you show up for your psychology study and you're told that you're either going to be building a replica of the Eiffel Tower out of wafer cookies or building a different tower using spaghetti and marshmallows. That is my kind of study.

Diehl and her colleagues have a twist, though: some of the participants only watched someone else build the tower while they took photos on their smartphone camera ("observers"); other participants actually built the tower while taking photos ("builders").

There were also groups of participants who observed and were asked not to take photos and those who were builders who also were asked not to take photos. Yea, a lot of groups. This was an ambitious study. Everyone filled out a survey to find out how engaging the experience was to them. So what did they find? Here's a breakdown of the main findings:

- Not surprisingly, if you were observing the building process and taking photos it was fun, but not very engaging. After all, you were just watching.
- However, observing and taking photos was a little more engaging than just standing there watching.
- If you were a builder, it was less engaging to have to also take photos while you were building.
- However, although builders who were told to take photos were a little distracted by having to do so, they found the activity as engaging as did the builders who didn't take photos.

Conclusion: taking photos while you're actively engaged in an activity doesn't decrease your engagement in the activity.

Let's get some wafer cookies and do this!

## LET'S TRY IT!

This study had a lot of groups. Let's just use the part of the study in which people built a wafer-cookie Eiffel Tower, with some asked to take pictures as they went along and others asked not to use their cameras. This way we'll find out if using your camera really does detract from your enjoyment. Here's what you'll need:

- Lots of wafer cookies
- Participants who all own cell phones with a built-in camera. You'll be dividing your participants into two groups—those who you'll allow to take photos with their cameras and those who will not be allowed to do this.
- Big room with tables

- Piece of paper for each participant to fill out when the activity is done

**WHAT TO DO:**

- **STEP 1:** Apparently, creating an Eiffel Tower out of wafers is quite common. To find out exactly what you need, do a web search on this phrase: "how to make eiffel tower out of wafers." You'll find lots of specific instructions. Print out the instructions for your participants.

- **STEP 2:** You'll want to run your "no photo" participants all at one time in the big room. Give them the instructions on how to build a tower and ask them not to take photos even if they are tempted to do so.

- **STEP 3:** When everyone's tower is done (Diehl gave her participants about twelve minutes), give everyone the following survey questions (individually) printed out on a sheet of paper.

How much did you enjoy the craft experience?

Did not enjoy it at all   **1   2   3   4   5   6   7**   Enjoyed it very much

To what extent did you feel you were really part of the craft experience?

**0   10   20   30   40   50   60   70   80   90   100**

| Felt I was not at all | Felt I was entirely |
|---|---|
| part of the experience | part of the experience |

To what extent did you feel immersed in the craft experience?

Not at all immersed   **1   2   3   4   5   6   7**   Extremely immersed

- **STEP 4:** After the participants circle their answers to these questions, remember to tell them what the whole study is about. Also, don't forget to put a "code" on the back of each survey so you'll know later which group each person was in (perhaps "NP" for those not allowed to take photos and "P" for those allowed).

- **STEP 5:** After your "no photo" participants have left, bring your "photo-taking" participants into the same room all at one time and follow the same directions as for the first group, except that you're going to tell them to build the tower and click away.

## THE RESULTS

If Diehl is right (and therefore many adults are wrong) you should find no difference between the two groups. It will be interesting to see if those who were allowed to take photos found the experience less immersive. Remember that Diehl's study has not yet been replicated (you may be the first), so we don't know how it'll come out when other researchers do it.

## WHY IT MATTERS

Taking photos with our smartphones is a behavior that is not going to go away. Everyone loves doing it. Smartphones are a normal part of just about everyone's life today, whether we like that or not, so we need to be clear about what effect the phones are having in our lives. We know without a doubt that texting while driving is dangerous, but do we know for sure if taking pictures when you're at an event really does take away from our enjoyment? These and other questions related to cell phones need investigation.

# BIBLIOGRAPHY

Ariely, D., G. Loewenstein, and D. Prelec. "'Coherent Arbitrariness': Stable Demand Curves Without Stable Preferences." *The Quarterly Journal of Economics* 118, no. 1 (2003): 73–106. doi:10.1162/00335530360535153.

Asch, Solomon E. "Group Forces in the Modification and Distortion of Judgments." *Social Psychology* (1952): 450–501. doi:10.1037/10025-016.

Barrett, Deirdre. *Supernormal Stimuli: How Primal Urges Overran Their Evolutionary Purpose.* New York: W.W. Norton & Company, 2010.

Burger, Jerry M. "Replicating Milgram: Would People Still Obey Today?" *American Psychologist* 64, no. 1 (2009): 1–11. doi:10.1037/a0010932.

Burnham, Clarke A. "Decrement of the Müller-Lyer Illusion with Saccadic and Tracking Eye Movements." *Perception & Psychophysics* 3, no. 6 (1968): 424–26. doi:10.3758/bf03205749.

Chabris, Christopher F., and Daniel J. Simons. *The Invisible Gorilla: And Other Ways Our Intuitions Deceive Us.* New York: Crown, 2010.

Cialdini, Robert B., et al. "Reciprocal Concessions Procedure for Inducing Compliance: The Door-in-the-Face Technique." *Journal of*

*Personality and Social Psychology* 31, no. 2 (1975): 206–15. doi:10.1037/h0076284.

Craik, Fergus I. M., and Endel Tulving. "Depth of Processing and the Retention of Words in Episodic Memory." *Journal of Experimental Psychology*: General 104, no. 3 (1975): 268–94. doi:10.1037/0096-3445.104.3.268.

Damisch, L., B. Stoberock, and T. Mussweiler. "Keep Your Fingers Crossed!: How Superstition Improves Performance." *Psychological Science* 21, no. 7 (2010): 1014–020. doi:10.1177/0956797610372631.

Darley, John M., and C. Daniel Batson. "'From Jerusalem to Jericho': A Study of Situational and Dispositional Variables in Helping Behavior." *Journal of Personality and Social Psychology* 27, no. 1 (1973): 100–08. doi:10.1037/h0034449.

De Beni, Rossana, and Cesare Cornoldi. "Does The Repeated Use Of Loci Create Interference?" *Perceptual and Motor Skills* 67, no. 2 (1988): 415–18. doi:10.2466/pms.1988.67.2.415.

Diehl, Kristin, Gal Zauberman, and Alixandra Barasch. "How Taking Photos Increases Enjoyment of Experiences." *Journal of Personality and Social Psychology*, 2016. doi:10.1037/pspa0000055.

Dion, Karen, Ellen Berscheid, and Elaine Walster. "What Is Beautiful Is Good." *Journal of Personality and Social Psychology* 24, no. 3 (1972): 285–90. doi:10.1037/h0033731.

Djordjevic, Sanja, and Hans Ijzerman. "Weight As an Embodiment of Importance: Replication and Extensions." *SSRN* Electronic Journal. doi:10.2139/ssrn.2586261.

Drews, Frank A., Monisha Pasupathi, and David L. Strayer. "Passenger and Cell Phone Conversations in Simulated Driving." *Journal of Experimental Psychology: Applied* 14, no. 4 (2008): 392–400. doi:10.1037/a0013119.

Eastwick, Paul W., and Wendi L. Gardner. "Is It a Game? Evidence for Social Influence in the Virtual World." *Social Influence* 4, no. 1 (2009): 18–32. doi:10.1080/15534510802254087.

Ebbinghaus, Hermann. *Memory: A Contribution to Experimental Psychology*. New York: Dover Publications, 1964.

Ekman, Paul, and Wallace V. Friesen. "Constants Across Cultures in the Face and Emotion." *Journal of Personality and Social Psychology* 17, no. 2 (1971): 124–29. doi:10.1037/h0030377.

Elliot, Andrew J., and Daniela Niesta. "Romantic Red: Red Enhances Men's Attraction to Women." *Journal of Personality and Social Psychology* 95, no. 5 (2008): 1150–164. doi:10.1037/0022-3514.95.5.1150.

Festinger, Leon, Henry W. Riecken, and Stanley Schachter. *When Prophecy Fails*. 1956. doi:10.1037/10030-000.

Festinger, Leon, and James M. Carlsmith. "Cognitive Consequences of Forced Compliance." *The Journal of Abnormal and Social Psychology* 58, no. 2 (1959): 203–10. doi:10.1037/h0041593.

Gilligan, Carol. *In a Different Voice: Women's Conceptions of Self and of Morality*. New York: Routledge, 1997.

Glucksberg, Sam. "The Influence of Strength of Drive on Functional Fixedness and Perceptual Recognition." *Journal of Experimental Psychology* 63, no. 1 (1962): 36–41. doi:10.1037/h0044683.

Granello, Darcy Haag, and Todd A. Gibbs. "The Power of Language and Labels: 'The Mentally Ill' versus 'People with Mental Illnesses.'" *Journal of Counseling & Development* 94, no. 1 (2016): 31–40. doi:10.1002/jcad.12059.

Hackman, J. Richard, and Greg R. Oldham. *Motivation through the Design of Work: Test of a Theory*. New Haven, CT: Yale University, Dept. of Administrative Sciences, 1974.

Haney, C., Banks, W. C., and Zimbardo, P. G. "A Study of Prisoners and Guards in a Simulated Prison." *Naval Research Reviews*, Office of Naval Research, 1973.

Hansen, Christine H., and Ranald D. Hansen. "Finding the Face in the Crowd: An Anger Superiority Effect." *Journal of Personality and Social Psychology* 54, no. 6 (1988): 917–24. doi:10.1037/0022-3514.54.6.917.

Harlow, Harry F. "The Nature of Love." *American Psychologist*, 13(12), Dec. 1958, 673–685.

Haught-Tromp, Catrinel. "The Green Eggs and Ham Hypothesis: How Constraints Facilitate Creativity." *Psychology of Aesthetics, Creativity, and the Arts*, 2016. doi:10.1037/aca0000061.

Herzberg, Frederick. *Job Attitudes: Review of Research and Opinion.* Pittsburgh, 1957.

Hunt, Morton M. *The Story of Psychology.* New York: Doubleday, 1993.

Jostmann, Nils B., Daniël Lakens, and Thomas W. Schubert. "Weight As an Embodiment of Importance." *Psychological Science* 20, no. 9 (2009): 1169–174. doi:10.1111/j.1467-9280.2009.02426.x.

Kang, Min Jeong, Ming Hsu, Ian M. Krajbich, George Loewenstein, Samuel M. McClure, Joseph Tao-yi Wang, and Colin F. Camerer. "The Wick in the Candle of Learning: Epistemic Curiosity Activates Reward Circuitry and Enhances Memory." *Psychological Science* 20, no. 8 (2009): 963–73. doi:10.1111/j.1467-9280.2009.02402.x.

Kohlberg, Lawrence. "The Development of Modes of Thinking and Choices in Years 10 to 16." Dissertation Thesis, 1958.

Larsson, A., N. Hooper, L. A. Osborne, P. Bennett, and L. McHugh. "Using Brief Cognitive Restructuring and Cognitive Defusion Techniques to Cope with Negative Thoughts." *Behavior Modification* 40, no. 3 (2015): 452–82. doi:10.1177/0145445515621488.

Latham, Gary P., and Gary A. Yukl. "Assigned versus Participative Goal Setting with Educated and Uneducated Woods Workers." *Journal of Applied Psychology* 60, no. 3 (1975): 299–302. doi:10.1037/h0076753.

Loftus, Elizabeth F., and John C. Palmer. "Reconstruction of Automobile Destruction: An Example of the Interaction between Language and Memory." *Journal of Verbal Learning and Verbal Behavior* 13, no. 5 (1974): 585–89. doi:10.1016/s0022-5371(74)80011-3.

Luchins, A. S. "Classroom Experiments on Mental Set." *The American Journal of Psychology* 59, no. 2 (1946): 295. doi:10.2307/1416894.

Maier, S. F., and M. E. Seligman. (2016). "Learned Helplessness at Fifty: Insights from Neuroscience." *Psychological Review*, 123 (4), 349–367. doi:10.1037/rev0000033.

McCabe, David P., and Alan D. Castel. "Seeing Is Believing: The Effect of Brain Images on Judgments of Scientific Reasoning." *Cognition* 107, no. 1 (2008): 343–52. doi:10.1016/j.cognition.2007.07.017.

Michael, Robert B., Eryn J. Newman, Matti Vuorre, Geoff Cumming, and Maryanne Garry. "On the (Non)Persuasive Power of a Brain Image." *Psychonomic Bulletin & Review* 20, no. 4 (2013): 720–25. doi:10.3758/s13423-013-0391-6.

Middlemist, R. Dennis, Eric S. Knowles, and Charles F. Matter. "Personal Space Invasions in the Lavatory: Suggestive Evidence for Arousal." *Journal of Personality and Social Psychology* 33, no. 5 (1976): 541–46. doi:10.1037/0022-3514.33.5.541.

Milgram, S. "Some Conditions of Obedience and Disobedience to Authority." *Human Relations* 18, no. 1 (1965): 57–76. doi:10.1177/001872676501800105.

Miller, George A. "The Magical Number Seven, Plus or Minus Two: Some Limits on Our Capacity for Processing Information." *Psychological Review* 101, no. 2 (1994): 343–52. doi:10.1037/0033-295x.101.2.343.

Norman, Donald A. *The Design of Everyday Things.* New York: Basic Books, 2002.

Oppenheimer, Daniel M. "Consequences of Erudite Vernacular Utilized Irrespective of Necessity: Problems with Using Long Words Needlessly." *Applied Cognitive Psychology* 20, no. 2 (2006): 139–56. doi:10.1002/acp.1178.

Pavlov, Ivan Petrovich, and William Henry Thompson. *The Work of the Digestive Glands.* London: C. Griffin, 1910.

Piaget, Jean. *The Origins of Intelligence in Children.* New York: International Universities Press, 1952.

Radvansky, Gabriel A., and David E. Copeland. "Walking Through Doorways Causes Forgetting: Situation Models and Experienced Space." *Memory & Cognition* 34, no. 5 (2006): 1150–156. doi:10.3758/bf03193261.

Reicher, S. D. and S. A. Haslam. "Rethinking the Psychology of Tyranny: The BBC Prison Study." *British Journal of Social Psychology*, 45, (2006): 1–40.

Rind, Bruce, and David Strohmetz. "Effect on Restaurant Tipping of Presenting Customers with an Interesting Task and of Reciprocity." *Journal of Applied Social Psychology* 31, no. 7 (2001): 1379–384. doi:10.1111/j.1559-1816.2001.tb02678.x.

Roediger, Henry L., and Kathleen B. McDermott. "Creating False Memories: Remembering Words Not Presented in Lists." *Journal of Experimental Psychology: Learning, Memory, and Cognition* 21, no. 4 (1995): 803–14. doi:10.1037/0278-7393.21.4.803.

Rorschach, Hermann. *Psychodiagnostik.* Bern: Huber, 1948.

Rose, Susan A., and Marion Blank. "The Potency of Context in Children's Cognition: An Illustration Through Conservation." *Child Development* 45, no. 2 (1974): 499. doi:10.2307/1127977.

Rosenhan, D. L. "On Being Sane in Insane Places."
*Perspectives in Abnormal Behavior*, 1974, 509-24. doi:10.1016/
b978-0-08-017738-0.50055-7.

Sagarin, Brad J., Robert B. Cialdini, William E. Rice, and
Sherman B. Serna. "Dispelling the Illusion of Invulnerability: The
Motivations and Mechanisms of Resistance to Persuasion." *Journal
of Personality and Social Psychology* 83, no. 3 (2002): 526-41.
doi:10.1037/0022-3514.83.3.526.

Seligman, Martin E., and Steven F. Maier. "Failure to Escape Traumatic
Shock." *Journal of Experimental Psychology* 74, no. 1 (1967): 1-9.
doi:10.1037/h0024514.

Sherif, Muzafer. *Experimental Study of Positive and Negative Intergroup
Attitudes Between Experimentally Produced Groups: Robbers Cave Study.*
Norman, OK, 1954.

Simons, Daniel J., and Daniel T. Levin. "Failure to Detect Changes to
People During a Real-World Interaction." *Psychonomic Bulletin & Review*
5, no. 4 (1998): 644-49. doi:10.3758/bf03208840.

Skinner, B. F. "'Superstition' in the Pigeon." *Journal of Experimental
Psychology* 38, no. 2 (1948): 168-72. doi:10.1037/h0055873.

Soussignan, Robert. "Duchenne Smile, Emotional Experience, and
Autonomic Reactivity: A Test of the Facial Feedback Hypothesis."
*Emotion* 2, no. 1 (2002): 52-74. doi:10.1037/1528-3542.2.1.52.

Stefanucci, Jeanine K., and Dennis R. Proffitt. "The Roles of Altitude and
Fear in the Perception of Height." *Journal of Experimental Psychology:
Human Perception and Performance*, Vol. 35(2), Apr. 2009, 424-438.

Tajfel, Henri. "Experiments in Intergroup Discrimination." *Scientific
American* 223, no. 5 (1970): 96-102. doi:10.1038/scientificamerican
1170-96.

Tifferet, Sigal, Daniel J. Kruger, Orly Bar-Lev, and Shani Zeller. "Dog Ownership Increases Attractiveness and Attenuates Perceptions of Short-Term Mating Strategy in Cad-Like Men." *Journal of Evolutionary Psychology* 11, no. 3 (2013): 121–29. doi:10.1556/jep.11.2013.3.2.

Tinbergen, Nikolaas. *The Study of Instinct*. Oxford: Clarendon Press, 1951.

Tversky, Amos, and Daniel Kahneman. *Rational Choice and the Framing of Decisions*. Ft. Belvoir: Defense Technical Information Center, 1986.

Van Boven, Leaf, and Thomas Gilovich. "To Do or to Have? That Is the Question." *Journal of Personality and Social Psychology* 85, no. 6 (2003): 1193–202. doi:10.1037/0022-3514.85.6.1193.

Vrij, Aldert, Sharon Leal, Samantha Mann, Lara Warmelink, Par Anders Granhag, and Ronald P. Fisher. "Drawings As an Innovative and Successful Lie Detection Tool." *Applied Cognitive Psychology*, 2009. doi:10.1002/acp.1627.

Williams, L. E., and J. A. Bargh. "Experiencing Physical Warmth Promotes Interpersonal Warmth." *Science* 322, no. 5901 (2008): 606–07. doi:10.1126/science.1162548.

Wiseman, Richard. *Quirkology: How We Discover the Big Truths in Small Things*. New York: Basic Books, 2007.

Zimbardo, P. G. "The Human Choice: Individuation, Reason, and Order versus Deindividuation, Impulse, and Chaos." *Nebraska Symposium on Motivation*, Vol. 17, (1969): 237–307.

# INDEX